Urne-Burial

Sir Thomas Browne
1605–1682

Sir Thomas Browne

Urne-Burial

PENGUIN BOOKS — GREAT IDEAS

PENGUIN BOOKS

Published by the Penguin Group
Penguin Books Ltd, 80 Strand, London WC2R ORL, England
Penguin Group (USA) Inc., 375 Hudson Street, New York, New York 10014, USA
Penguin Group (Canada), 10 Alcorn Avenue, Toronto, Ontario, Canada M4V 3B2
(a division of Pearson Penguin Canada Inc.)
Penguin Ireland, 25 St Stephen's Green, Dublin 2, Ireland
(a division of Penguin Books Ltd)
Penguin Group (Australia), 250 Camberwell Road,
Camberwell, Victoria 3124, Australia (a division of Pearson Australia Group Pty Ltd)
Penguin Books India Pvt Ltd, 11 Community Centre,
Panchsheel Park, New Delhi – 110 017, India
Penguin Group (NZ), cnr Airborne and Rosedale Roads, Albany,
Auckland 1310, New Zealand (a division of Pearson New Zealand Ltd)
Penguin Books (South Africa) (Pty) Ltd, 24 Sturdee Avenue,
Rosebank 2196, South Africa

Penguin Books Ltd, Registered Offices: 80 Strand, London WC2R ORL, England

www.penguin.com

The Major Works first published in Penguin Classics 1977
These extracts first published in Penguin Books 2005

1

Taken from the Penguin Classics edition *The Major Works*,
edited by C. A. Patrides

Set by Rowland Phototypesetting Ltd, Bury St Edmunds, Suffolk
Printed in England by Clays Ltd, St Ives plc

Contents

A Note on the Text

The possibly reckless decision has been taken that, despite Browne's obscurities, this edition should maintain the *Great Ideas* pattern of minimal annotations. All Latin has been translated and some of Browne's own footnotes to *Urne-Burial* kept, but readers are otherwise on their own. Even in his lifetime Browne's allusions and vocabulary must have offered challenges, but then as now the rewards are very great.

Hydriotaphia: Urne-Burial or, A Brief Discourse of the Sepulchrall Urnes Lately Found in Norfolk

Chapter I

In the deep discovery of the Subterranean world, a shallow part would satisfie some enquirers; who, if two or three yards were open about the surface, would not care to rake the bowels of *Potosi*,* and regions towards the Centre. Nature hath furnished one part of the Earth, and man another. The treasures of time lie high, in Urnes, Coynes, and Monuments, scarce below the roots of some vegetables. Time hath endlesse rarities, and shows of all varieties; which reveals old things in heaven, makes new discoveries in earth, and even earth it self a discovery. That great Antiquity *America* lay buried for thousands of years; and a large part of the earth is still in the Urne unto us.

Though if *Adam* were made out of an extract of the Earth, all parts might challenge a restitution, yet few have returned their bones farre lower than they might receive them; not affecting the graves of Giants, under hilly and heavy coverings, but content with lesse than their owne depth, have wished their bones might lie soft,

* The rich mountain of *Peru*. [All footnotes are Browne's.]

I

and the earth be light upon them; Even such as hope to rise again, would not be content with centrall interrment, or so desperately to place their reliques as to lie beyond discovery, and in no way to be seen again; which happy contrivance hath made communication with our forefathers, and left unto our view some parts, which they never beheld themselves.

Though earth hath engrossed the name yet water hath proved the smartest grave; which in forty dayes swallowed almost mankinde, and the living creation; Fishes not wholly escaping, except the Salt Ocean were handsomely contempered by admixture of the fresh Element.

Many have taken voluminous pains to determine the state of the soul upon disunion; but men have been most phantasticall in the singular contrivances of their corporall dissolution; whilest the sobrest Nations have rested in two wayes, of simple inhumation and burning.

That carnall interment or burying, was of the elder date, the old examples of *Abraham* and the Patriarchs are sufficient to illustrate; And were without competition, if it could be made out, that *Adam* was buried near *Damascus*, or Mount *Calvary*, according to some Tradition. God himself, that buried but one, was pleased to make choice of this way, collectible from Scripture-expression, and the hot contest between Satan and the Arch-Angel, about discovering the body of *Moses*. But the practice of Burning was also of great Antiquity, and of no slender extent. For (not to derive the same from *Hercules*) noble descriptions there are hereof in the Grecian Funerals of *Homer*, In the formall Obsequies of *Patroclus*, and *Achilles*; and somewhat elder in the *Theban* warre, and solemn combustion of *Meneceus*, and *Archemorus*, contemporary unto *Jair* the Eighth Judge of *Israel*. Confirmable also among the *Trojans*, from the Funerall Pyre of *Hector*, burnt before the gates of *Troy*, And the burning of *Penthisilea* the *Amazonean Queen*: and long continuance of that practice, in the inward Countries of *Asia*; while as low as the Reign of *Julian*, we finde that the King of *Chionia* burnt the body of his Son, and interred the ashes in a silver Urne.

The same practice extended also farre West, and besides *Herulians*, *Getes*, and *Thracians*, was in use with most of the *Celtæ*, *Sarmatians*, *Germans*, *Gauls*, *Danes*, *Swedes*, *Norwegians*; not to omit some use thereof among *Carthaginians* and *Americans*: Of greater Antiquity among the *Romans* than most opinion, or *Pliny* seems to allow. For (beside the old Table Laws of burning or burying within the City, of making the Funerall fire with plained wood, or quenching the fire with wine) *Manlius* the Consul burnt the body of his Son: *Numa* by speciall clause of his Will, was not burnt but buried; And *Remus* was solemnly burned, according to the description of *Ovid*.

Cornelius Sylla was not the first whose body was burned in *Rome*, but of the *Cornelian* Family, which being indifferently, not frequently used before, from that time spread, and became the prevalent practice. Not totally pursued in the highest runne of Cremation; For when even Crows were funerally burnt, *Poppæa* the Wife of *Nero* found a peculiar grave enterment. Now as all customes were founded upon some bottome of Reason, so there wanted not grounds for this; according to severall apprehensions of the most rationall dissolution. Some being of the opinion of *Thales*, that water was the originall of all things, thought it most equall to submit unto the principle of putrefaction, and conclude in a moist relentment. Others conceived it most natural to end in fire, as due unto the master principle in the composition, according to the doctrine of *Heraclitus*. And therefore heaped up large piles, more actively to waft them toward that Element, whereby they also declined a visible degeneration into worms, and left a lasting parcell of their composition.

Some apprehended a purifying virtue in fire, refining the grosser commixture, and firing out the Æthereall particles so deeply immersed in it. And such as by tradition or rationall conjecture held any hint of the finall pyre of all things; or that this Element at last must be too hard for all the rest; might conceive most naturally of the fiery dissolution. Others pretending no natural grounds, politickly declined the malice of enemies upon their buried bodies. Which consideration led *Sylla* unto this practise; who having thus served the body of *Marius*, could not but fear a retaliation upon his own, entertained after in the Civill wars, and revengeful contentions of *Rome*.

But as many Nations embraced, and many left it indifferent, so others too much affected, or strictly declined this practice. The *Indian Brachmans* seemed too great friends unto fire, who burnt themselves alive, and thought it the noblest way to end their dayes in fire; according to the expression of the Indian, burning himself at *Athens*, in his last words upon the pyre unto the amazed spectators, *Thus I make my selfe Immortall*.

But the *Chaldeans*, the great Idolaters of fire, abhorred the burning of their carcasses, as a pollution of that Deity. The *Persian Magi* declined it upon the like scruple, and being only sollicitous about their bones, exposed their flesh to the prey of Birds and Dogges. And the *Persees* now in *India*, which expose their bodies unto Vultures, and endure not so much as *feretra* or Beers of Wood, the proper Fuell of fire, are led on with such niceties. But whether the ancient *Germans* who burned their dead, held any such fear to pollute their Deity of *Herthus*, or the earth, we have no Authentick conjecture.

The Ægyptians were afraid of fire, not as a Deity, but a devouring Element, mercilesly consuming their bodies, and leaving too little of them; and therefore by precious Embalments, depositure in dry earths, or handsome inclosure in glasses, contrived the notablest wayes of integrall conservation. And from such Ægyptian scruples imbibed by *Pythagoras*, it may be conjectured that *Numa* and the Pythagoricall Sect first waved the fiery solution.

The *Scythians* who swore by winde and sword, that is, by life and death, were so farre from burning their bodies, that they declined all interrment, and made their graves in the ayr: And the *Ichthyophagi* or fish-eating Nations about Ægypt, affected the Sea for their grave: Thereby declining visible corruption, and restoring the debt of their bodies. Whereas the old Heroes in *Homer* dread nothing more than water or drowning; probably upon the old opinion of the fiery substance of the soul, only extinguishable by that Element; And therefore the Poet emphatically implieth the totall destruction in this kinde of death, which happened to *Ajax Oileus*.

The old *Balearians* had a peculiar mode, for they used great Urnes and much wood, but no fire in their burials, while they bruised the flesh and bones of the dead, crowded them into Urnes, and laid heapes of wood upon them. And the *Chinois* without cremation or urnall interrment of their bodies, make use of trees and much burning, while they plant a Pine-tree by their grave, and burn great numbers of printed draughts of slaves and horses over it, civilly content with their companies in effigie, which barbarous Nations exact unto reality.

Christians abhorred this way of obsequies, and though they stickt not to give their bodies to be burnt in their lives, detested that mode after death; affecting rather a depositure than absumption, and properly submitting unto the sentence of God, to return not unto ashes but unto dust againe, conformable unto the practice of the Patriarchs, the interrment of our Saviour, of *Peter*, *Paul*, and the ancient Martyrs. And so farre at last declining promiscuous enterrment with Pagans, that some have suffered Ecclesiastical censures, for making no scruple thereof.

The *Musselman* beleevers will never admit this fiery resolution. For they hold a present trial from their black and white Angels in the grave; which they must have made so hollow, that they may rise upon their knees.

The Jewish Nation, though they entertained the old way of inhumation, yet sometimes admitted this practice. For the men of *Jabesh* burnt the body of *Saul*. And by no prohibited practice, to avoid contagion or pollution, in time of pestilence, burnt the bodies of their friends. And when they burnt not their dead bodies, yet sometimes used great burnings neare and about them, deducible from the expressions concerning *Jeboram*, *Sedechias*, and the sumptuous pyre of *Asa*: And were so little averse from Pagan burning, that the Jews lamenting the death of *Cæsar* their friend, and revenger on *Pompey*, frequented the place where his body was burnt for many nights together. And as they raised noble Monuments and *Mausolæums* for their own Nation, so they were not scrupulous in erecting some for others, according to the practice of *Daniel*, who left that lasting sepulchrall pyle in *Echbatana*, for the *Medean* and *Persian* Kings.

But even in times of subjection and hottest use, they conformed not unto the *Romane* practice of burning; whereby the Prophecy was secured concerning the body of Christ, that it should not see corruption, or a bone should not be broken; which we beleeve was also providentially prevented, from the Souldiers spear and nails that past by the little bones both in his hands and feet: Nor of ordinary contrivance, that it should not corrupt on the Crosse, according to the Laws of *Romane* Crucifixion, or an hair of his head perish, though observable in Jewish customes, to cut the hairs of Malefactors.

Nor in their long co-habitation with Ægyptians, crept into a custome of their exact embalming, wherein deeply slashing the muscles, and taking out the brains and entrails, they had broken the subject of so entire a Resurrection, nor fully answered the types of *Enoch*, *Eliah*, or *Jonah*, which yet to prevent or restore, was of equall facility unto that rising power, able to break the fasciations and bands of death, to get clear out of the Cere-cloth, and an hundred pounds of oyntment, and out of the Sepulchre before the stone was rolled from it.

But though they embraced not this practice of burning, yet entertained they many ceremonies agreeable unto *Greeke* and *Romane* obsequies. And he that observeth their funerall Feasts, their Lamentations at the grave, their musick, and weeping mourners; how they closed the eyes of their friends, how they washed, anointed, and kissed the dead; may easily conclude these were not meere Pagan-Civilities. But whether that mournfull burthen, and treble calling out after *Absalom*, had any reference unto the last conclamation, and triple valediction, used by other Nations, we hold but a wavering conjecture.

Civilians make sepulture but of the Law of Nations, others doe naturally found it and discover it also in animals. They that are so thick skinned as still to credit the story of the *Phœnix*, may say something for animall burning: More serious conjectures finde some examples of sepulture in Elephants, Cranes, the Sepulchrall Cells of Pismires and practice of Bees; which civill society carrieth out their dead, and hath exequies, if not interrments.

Chapter II

The Solemnities, Ceremonies, Rites of their Cremation or enterrment, so solemnly delivered by Authours, we shall not disparage our Reader to repeat. Only the last and lasting part in their Urns, collected bones and Ashes, we cannot wholly omit, or decline that Subject, which occasion lately presented, in some discovered among us.

In a Field of old *Walsingham*, not many moneths past, were digged up between fourty and fifty Urnes, deposited in a dry and sandy soile, not a yard deep, nor farre from one another: Not all strictly of one figure, but most answering these described: Some containing two pounds of bones, distinguishable in skulls, ribs, jawes, thigh-bones, and teeth, with fresh impressions of their combustion. Besides the extraneous substances, like peeces of small boxes, or combes handsomely wrought, handles of small brasse instruments, brazen nippers, and in one some kinde of *Opale*.

Near the same plot of ground, for about six yards compasse were digged up coals and incinerated substances, which begat conjecture that this was the *Ustrina* or place of burning their bodies, or some sacrificing place unto the *Manes*, which was properly below the surface of the ground, as the *Aræ* and Altars unto the gods and *Heroes* above it.

That these were the Urnes of *Romanes* from the common custome and place where they were found, is no obscure conjecture, not farre from a *Romane* Garrison, and but five Miles from *Brancaster*, set down by ancient Record under the name of *Brannodunum*. And where the adjoyning Towne, containing seven Parishes, in no very different sound, but Saxon Termination, still retains the Name of *Burnham*, which being an early station, it is not improbable the neighbour parts were filled with habitations, either of *Romanes* themselves, or *Brittains Romanised*, which observed the *Romane* customes.

Nor is it improbable that the *Romanes* early possessed this Countrey; for though we meet not with such strict

En Sum quod digitis Quinque Levatur onus Propert:

particulars of these parts, before the new Institution of
Constantine, and military charge of the Count of the
Saxon shore, and that about the *Saxon* Invasions, the
Dalmatian Horsemen were in the Garrison of *Brancaster*:
Yet in the time of *Claudius*, *Vespasian*, and *Severus*, we
finde no lesse than three Legions dispersed through the
Province of *Brittain*. And as high as the Reign of *Claudius*
a great overthrow was given unto the *Iceni*, by the
Romane Lieutenant *Ostorius*. Not long after the Countrey
was so molested, that in hope of a better state, *Prasutagus*
bequeathed his Kingdome unto *Nero* and his Daughters;
and *Boadicea* his Queen fought the last decisive Battle
with *Paulinus*. After which time and Conquest of *Agricola*
the Lieutenant of *Vespasian*, probable it is they wholly
possessed this Countrey, ordering it into Garrisons or
Habitations, best suitable with their securities. And
so some *Romane* Habitations, not improbable in these
parts, as high as the time of *Vespasian*, where the *Saxons*
after seated, in whose thin-fill'd Mappes we yet finde
the Name of *Walsingham*. Now if the *Iceni* were but
Gammadims, *Anconians*, or men that lived in an Angle
wedge or Elbow of *Brittain*, according to the Originall
Etymologie, this countrey will challenge the Emphaticall
appellation, as most properly making the Elbow or Iken
of *Icenia*.

That *Britain* was notably populous is undeniable, from
that expression of *Cæsar*. That the *Romans* themselves
were early in no small Numbers, Seventy Thousand with
their associats slain by *Boadicea*, affords a sure account.
And though many *Roman* habitations are now un-
knowne, yet some by old works, Rampiers, Coynes, and

Urnes doe testifie their Possessions. Some Urnes have been found at *Castor*, some also about *Southcreake*, and not many years past, no lesse than ten in a Field at *Buxton*, not near any recorded Garison. Nor is it strange to finde *Romane* Coynes of Copper and Silver among us; of *Vespasian*, *Trajan*, *Adrian*, *Commodus*, *Antoninus*, *Severus*, &c. But the greater number of *Dioclesian*, *Constantine*, *Constans*, *Valens*, with many of *Victorinus*, *Posthumius*, *Tetricus*, and the thirty Tyrants in the Reigne of *Gallienus*; and some as high as *Adrianus* have been found about *Thetford*, or *Sitomagus*, mentioned in the itinerary of *Antoninus*, as the way from *Venta* or *Castor* unto *London*. But the most frequent discovery is made at the two *Casters* by *Norwich* and *Tarmouth*, at *Burghcastle* and *Brancaster*.

Besides the *Norman*, *Saxon* and *Danish* peeces of *Cuthred*, *Canutus*, *William*, *Matilda*, and others, som British Coynes of gold have been dispersedly found; And no small number of silver peeces near *Norwich*; with a rude head upon the obverse, and an ill formed horse on the reverse, with Inscriptions *Ic. Duro. T.* whether implying *Iceni*, *Durotriges*, *Tascia*, or *Trinobantes*, we leave to higher conjecture. Vulgar Chronology will have *Norwich* Castle as old as *Julius Cæsar*; but his distance from these parts, and its *Gothick* form of structure, abridgeth such Antiquity. The *British* Coyns afford conjecture of early habitation in these parts, though the City of *Norwich* arose from the ruines of *Venta*, and though perhaps not without some habitation before, was enlarged, builded, and nominated by the *Saxons*. In what bulk or populosity it stood in the old East-angle Mon-

archy, tradition and history are silent. Considerable it
was in the *Danish* Eruptions, when *Sueno* burnt *Thetford*
and *Norwich*, and *Ulfketel* the Governour thereof was
able to make some resistance, and after endeavoured to
burn the *Danish* Navy.

How the *Romanes* left so many Coynes in Countreys
of their Conquests, seems of hard resolution, except we
consider how they buried them under ground, when
upon barbarous invasions they were fain to desert their
habitations in most part of their Empire; and the
strictnesse of their laws forbidding to transfer them to
any other uses; Wherein the *Spartans* were singular, who
to make their Copper money uselesse, contempered it
with vinegar. That the *Brittains* left any, some wonder;
since their money was iron, and Iron rings before *Cæsar*;
and those of after stamp by permission, and but small in
bulk and bignesse. That so few of the *Saxons* remain,
because overcome by succeeding Conquerours upon the
place, their Coynes by degrees passed into other stamps,
and the marks of after ages.

Than the time of these Urnes deposited, or precise
Antiquity of these Reliques, nothing of more uncertainty.
For since the Lieutenant of *Claudius* seems to have made
the first progresse into these parts, since *Boadicea* was
overthrown by the Forces of *Nero*, and *Agricola* put a full
end to these Conquests; it is not probable the Countrey
was fully garrison'd or planted before; and therefore
however these Urnes might be of later date, not likely
of higher Antiquity.

And the succeeding Emperours desisted not from their
Conquests in these and other parts; as testified by history

and medall inscription yet extant. The Province of *Brittain* is so divided a distance from *Rome*, beholding the faces of many Imperiall persons, and in large account no fewer than *Cæsar*, *Claudius*, *Britannicus*, *Vespasian*, *Titus*, *Adrian*, *Severus*, *Commodus*, *Geta*, and *Caracalla*.

A great obscurity herein, because no medall or Emperours Coyne enclosed, which might denote the date of their enterrments; observable in many Urnes, and found in those of *Spittle* Fields by *London*, which contained the Coynes of *Claudius*, *Vespasian*, *Commodus*, *Antoninus*, attended with Lacrymatories, Lamps, Bottles of Liquor, and other appurtenances of affectionate superstition, which in these rurall interrements were wanting.

Some uncertainty there is from the period or term of burning, or the cessation of that practise. *Macrobius* affirmeth it was disused in his dayes. But most agree, though without authentick record, that it ceased with the *Antonini*. Most safely to be understood, after the Reigne of those Emperours which assumed the name of *Antoninus*, extending unto *Heliogabalus*. Not strictly after *Marcus*; For about fifty years later we finde the magnificent burning, and consecration of *Severus*; and if we so fix this period or cessation, these Urnes will challenge above thirteen hundred years.

But whether this practise was onely then left by Emperours and great persons, or generally about *Rome*, and not in other Provinces, we hold no authentick account. For after *Tertullian*, in the dayes of *Minucius* it was obviously objected upon Christians, that they condemned the practise of burning. And we finde a passage in *Sidonius*, which asserteth that practise in *France* unto a lower account. And perhaps not fully disused till Christianity fully established, which gave the finall extinction to these sepulchrall Bonefires.

Whether they were the bones of men or women or children, no authentick decision from ancient custome in distinct places of buriall. Although not improbably conjectured, that the double Sepulture or burying place of *Abraham*, had in it such intension. But from exility of bones, thinnesse of skulls, smallnesse of teeth, ribbes, and thigh-bones; not improbable that many thereof were persons of *minor* age, or women. Confirmable also from things contained in them: In most were found substances resembling Combes, Plates like Boxes, fastened with Iron pins, and handsomely overwrought like the necks or Bridges of Musicall Instruments, long brasse plates over-wrought like the handles of neat implements, brazen nippers to pull away hair, and in one a kinde of *Opale* yet maintaining a blewish colour.

Now that they accustomed to burn or bury with them things wherein they excelled, delighted, or which were dear unto them, either as farewells unto all pleasure, or vain apprehension that they might use them in the other world, is testified by all Antiquity. Observable from the Gemme or Berill Ring upon the finger of *Cynthia*, the Mistresse of *Propertius*, when after her Funerall Pyre her Ghost appeared unto him. And notably illustrated from the Contents of that *Romane* Urne preserved by Cardinall *Farnese*, wherein besides great number of Gemmes with heads of Gods and Goddesses, were found an Ape of *Agath*, a Grashopper, an Elephant of Ambre, a Crystall Ball, three glasses, two Spoones, and six Nuts of Crystall.

And beyond the content of Urnes, in the Monument of
Childerick the first, and fourth King from *Pharamond*,
casually discovered three years past at *Tournay*, restoring
unto the world much gold richly adorning his Sword,
two hundred Rubies, many hundred Imperial Coyns,
three hundred golden Bees, the bones and horseshoe of
his horse enterred with him, according to the barbarous
magnificence of those dayes in their sepulchral Obsequies. Although if we steer by the conjecture of many
and Septuagint expression; some trace thereof may be
found even with the ancient Hebrews, not only from the
Sepulcrall treasure of *David*, but the circumcision knives
which *Josuah* also buried.

Some men considering the contents of these Urnes,
lasting peeces and toyes included in them, and the
custome of burning with many other Nations, might
somewhat doubt whether all Urnes found among us
were properly *Romane* Reliques, or some not belonging
unto our *British*, *Saxon*, or *Danish* Forefathers.

In the form of Buriall among the ancient *Brittains*, the
large Discourses of *Cæsar*, *Tacitus*, and *Strabo* are silent:
For the discovery whereof, with other particulars, we
much deplore the losse of that Letter which *Cicero*
expected or received from his Brother *Quintus*, as a
resolution of *Brittish* customes; or the account which
might have been made by *Scribonius Largus*, the Physician
accompanying the Emperour *Claudius*, who might have
also discovered that frugall Bit of the Old *Brittains*, which
in the bignesse of a Bean could satisfie their thirst and
hunger.

But that the *Druids* and ruling Priests used to burn

and bury, is expressed by *Pomponius*; That *Bellinus* the Brother of *Brennus* and King of *Brittains* was burnt, is acknowledged by *Polydorus*. That they held that practise in *Gallia*, *Cæsar* expresly delivereth. Whether the *Brittains* (probably descended from them, of like Religion, Language and Manners) did not sometimes make use of burning; or whether at least such as were after civilized unto the *Romane* life and manners, conformed not unto this practise, we have not historicall assertion or deniall. But since from the account of *Tacitus* the *Romanes* early wrought so much civility upon the British stock, that they brought them to build Temples, to wear the Gowne, and study the *Romane* Laws and language, that they conformed also unto their religious rites and customes in burials, seems no improbable conjecture.

That burning the dead was used in *Sarmatia*, is affirmed by *Gaguinus*, that the *Sueons* and *Gothlanders* used to burne their Princes and great persons, is delivered by *Saxo* and *Olaus*; that this was the old *Germane* practise, is also asserted by *Tacitus*. And though we are bare in historicall particulars of such obsequies in this Island, or that the *Saxons*, *Jutes*, and *Angles* burnt their dead, yet came they from parts where 'twas of ancient practise; the *Germanes* using it, from whom they were descended. And even in *Jutland* and *Sleswick* in *Anglia Cymbrica*, Urnes with bones were found not many years before us.

But the *Danish* and Northern Nations have raised an Æra or point of compute from their Custome of burning their dead: Some deriving it from *Unguinus*, some from *Frotho* the great; who ordained by Law, that Princes and

Chief Commanders should be committed unto the fire, though the common sort had the common grave enterrment. So *Starkatterus* that old *Heroe* was burnt, and *Ringo* royally burnt the body of *Harald* the King slain by him.

What time this custome generally expired in that Nation, we discern no assured period; whether it ceased before Christianity, or upon their Conversion, by *Ansgarius* the Gaul in the time of *Ludovicus Pius* the Sonne of *Charles* the great, according to good computes; or whether it might not be used by some persons, while for a hundred and eighty years Paganisme and Christianity were promiscuously embraced among them, there is no assured conclusion. About which times the *Danes* were busie in *England*, and particularly infested this Countrey: Where many Castles and strong holds were built by them, or against them, and great number of names and Families still derived from them. But since this custome was probably disused before their Invasion or Conquest, and the *Romanes* confessedly practised the same, since their possession of this Island, the most assured account will fall upon the *Romanes*, or *Brittains Romanized*.

However, certain it is, that Urnes conceived of no *Romane* Originall, are often digged up both in *Norway*, and *Denmark*, handsomely described, and graphically represented by the Learned Physician *Wormius*, And in some parts of *Denmark* in no ordinary number, as stands delivered by Authours exactly describing those Countreys. And they contained not only bones, but many other substances in them, as Knives, peeces of Iron, Brasse and Wood, and one of *Norwaye* a brasse guilded Jewes-harp.

Nor were they confused or carelesse in disposing the noblest sort, while they placed large stones in circle about the Urnes, or bodies which they interred: Somewhat answerable unto the Monument of *Rollrich* stones in England, or sepulcrall Monument probably erected by *Rollo*, who after conquered *Normandy*. Where 'tis not improbable somewhat might be discovered. Mean while to what Nation or person belonged that large Urne found at *Ashburie*, containing mighty bones, and a Buckler; What those large Urnes found at little *Massingham*, or why the *Anglesea* Urnes are placed with their mouths downward, remains yet undiscovered.

Chapter III

Playstered and whited Sepulchres were anciently affected in cadaverous and corruptive Burials; And the rigid Jews were wont to garnish the Sepulchres of the righteous; *Ulysses* in *Hecuba* cared not how meanly he lived, so he might finde a noble Tomb after death. Great Persons affected great Monuments, And the fair and larger Urnes contained no vulgar ashes, which makes that disparity in those which time discovereth among us. The present Urnes were not of one capacity, the largest containing above a gallon, Some not much above half that measure; nor all of one figure, wherein there is no strict conformity, in the same or different Countreys; Observable from those represented by *Casalius*, *Bosio*, and others, though all found in *Italy*: While many have handles, ears, and long necks, but most imitate a circular figure, in a sphericall and round composure; whether from any mystery, best duration or capacity, were but a conjecture. But the common form with necks was a proper figure, making our last bed like our first; nor much unlike the Urnes of our Nativity, while we lay in the nether part of the Earth, and inward vault of our Microcosme. Many Urnes are red, these but of a black colour, somewhat smooth, and dully sounding, which begat some doubt, whether they were burnt, or only baked in Oven or Sunne: According to the ancient way, in many bricks, tiles, pots, and testaceous works; and as the word *testa* is properly to be taken, when occurring without addition: And chiefly intended by *Pliny*, when he commendeth bricks and tiles of two years old, and to make them in the spring. Nor only these concealed peeces, but the open magnificence of Antiquity, ran much in the Artifice of Clay. Hereof the house of *Mausolus* was built, thus old *Jupiter* stood in the Capitoll, and the *Statua* of *Hercules* made in the Reign of *Tarquinius Priscus*, was extant in *Plinies* dayes. And such as declined burning or Funerall Urnes, affected Coffins of Clay, according to the mode of *Pythagoras*, and way preferred by *Varro*. But the spirit of great ones was above these circumscriptions, affecting copper, silver, gold, and *Porphyrie* Urnes, wherein *Severus* lay, after a serious view and sentence on that which should contain him. Some of these Urnes were thought to have been silvered over, from sparklings in several pots, with small Tinsell parcels; uncertain whether from the earth, or the first mixture in them.

Among these Urnes we could obtain no good account of their coverings; Only one seemed arched over with

some kinde of brickwork. Of those found at *Buxton* some
were covered with flints, some in other parts with tiles,
those at *Tarmouth Caster* were closed with *Romane* bricks.
And some have proper earthen covers adapted and fitted
to them. But in the *Homericall* Urne of *Patroclus*, whatever
was the solid Tegument, we finde the immediate cover-
ing to be a purple peece of silk: And such as had no
covers might have the earth closely pressed into them,
after which disposure were probably some of these,
wherein we found the bones and ashes half mortered
unto the sand and sides of the Urne; and some long roots
of Quich, or Dogs-grass wreathed about the bones.

No Lamps, included Liquors, Lachrymatories, or
Tearbottles attended these rurall Urnes, either as sacred
unto the *Manes*, or passionate expressions of their surviving friends. While with rich flames and hired tears they
solemnized their Obsequies, and in the most lamented
Monuments made one part of their Inscriptions. Some
finde sepulchrall Vessels containing liquors, which time
hath incrassated into gellies. For beside these Lachrymatories, notable Lamps with Vessels of Oyles and
Aromaticall Liquors attended noble Ossuaries. And some
yet retaining a Vinosity and spirit in them, which if
any have tasted they have farre exceeded the Palats of
Antiquity. Liquors not to be computed by years of
annuall Magistrates, but by great conjunctions and the
fatall periods of Kingdomes. The draughts of Consulary
date were but crude unto these, and *Opimian* Wine but
in the must unto them.

In sundry Graves and Sepulchres, we meet with Rings,
Coynes, and Chalices; Ancient frugality was so severe,

that they allowed no gold to attend the Corps, but only that which served to fasten their teeth. Whether the *Opaline* stone in this Urne were burnt upon the finger of the dead, or cast into the fire by some affectionate friend, it will consist with either custome. But other incinerable substances were found so fresh, that they could feel no sindge from fire. These upon view were judged to be wood, but sinking in water and tried by the fire, we found them to be bone or Ivory. In their hardnesse and yellow colour they most resembled Box, which in old expressions found the Epithete of Eternall, and perhaps in such conservatories might have passed uncorrupted.

That Bay-leaves were found green in the Tomb of S. *Humbert*, after an hundred and fifty years, was looked upon as miraculous. Remarkable it was unto old Spectators, that the Cypresse of the Temple of *Diana* lasted so many hundred years: The wood of the Ark and Olive Rod of *Aaron* were older at the Captivity. But the Cypresse of the Ark of *Noah* was the greatest vegetable Antiquity, if *Josephus* were not deceived by some fragments of it in his dayes. To omit the Moore-logs, and Firre-trees found under-ground in many parts of *England*; the undated ruines of windes, flouds or earthquakes; and which in *Flanders* still shew from what quarter they fell, as generally lying in a North-East position.

But though we found not these peeces to be Wood, according to first apprehension, yet we missed not altogether of some woody substance; For the bones were not so clearly pickt, but some coals were found amongst them; A way to make wood perpetuall, and a fit associat for metall, whereon was laid the foundation of the great

Ephesian Temple, and which were made the lasting tests of old boundaries and Landmarks; Whilest we look on these, we admire not Observations of Coals found fresh, after four hundred years. In a long deserted habitation, even Egge-shels have been found fresh, not tending to corruption.

In the Monument of King *Childerick*, the Iron Reliques were found all rusty and crumbling into peeces. But our little Iron pins which fastened the Ivory works, held well together, and lost not their Magneticall quality, though wanting a tenacious moisture for the firmer union of parts; although it be hardly drawn into fusion, yet that metall soon submitteth unto rust and dissolution. In the brazen peeces we admired not the duration but the freedome from rust and ill savour, upon the hardest attrition; but now exposed unto the piercing Atomes of ayre, in the space of a few moneths, they begin to spot and betray their green entrals. We conceive not these Urnes to have descended thus naked as they appear, or to have entred their graves without the old habit of flowers. The Urne of *Philopœmen* was so laden with flowers and ribbons, that it afforded no sight of it self. The rigid *Lycurgus* allowed Olive and Myrtle. The *Athenians* might fairly except against the practise of *Democritus* to be buried up in honey; as fearing to embezzle a great commodity of their Countrey, and the best of that kinde in *Europe*. But *Plato* seemed too frugally politick, who allowed no larger Monument than would contain four Heroick Verses, and designed the most barren ground for sepulture: Though we cannot commend the goodnesse of that sepulchrall ground, which was set at no higher rate than the mean salary of *Judas*. Though the earth had confounded the ashes of these Ossuaries, yet the bones were so smartly burnt, that some thin plates of brasse were found half melted among them; whereby we apprehend they were not of the meanest carcasses, perfunctorily fired as sometimes in military, and commonly in pestilence, burnings; or after the manner of abject corps, hudled forth and carelesly burnt, without the Esquiline Port at *Rome*; which was an affront contrived upon *Tiberius*, while they but half burnt his body, and in the Amphitheatre, according to the custome in notable Malefactors; whereas *Nero* seemed not so much to feare his death, as that his head should be cut off, and his body not burnt entire.

Some finding many fragments of sculs in these Urnes, suspected a mixture of bones; In none we searched was there cause of such conjecture, though sometimes they declined not that practise; The ashes of *Domitian* were mingled with those of *Julia*, of *Achilles* with those of *Patroclus*: All Urnes contained not single Ashes; Without confused burnings they affectionately compounded their bones; passionately endeavouring to continue their living Unions. And when distance of death denied such conjunctions, unsatisfied affections conceived some satisfaction to be neighbours in the grave, to lye Urne by Urne, and touch but in their names. And many were so curious to continue their living relations, that they contrived large, and family Urnes, wherein the Ashes of their nearest friends and kindred might successively be received, at least some parcels thereof, while their collaterall memorials lay in *minor* vessels about them.

Antiquity held too light thoughts from Objects of mortality, while some drew provocatives of mirth from Anatomies, and Juglers shewed tricks with Skeletons. When Fidlers made not so pleasant mirth as Fencers, and men could sit with quiet stomacks while hanging was plaied before them. Old considerations made few *memento's* by sculs and bones upon their monuments. In the Ægyptian Obelisks and Hieroglyphicall figures it is not easie to meet with bones. The sepulchrall Lamps speak nothing lesse than sepulture; and in their literall draughts prove often obscene and antick peeces: Where we finde *D.M.* it is obvious to meet with sacrificing *patera's*, and vessels of libation, upon old sepulchrall Monuments. In the Jewish *Hypogæum* and subterranean Cell at *Rome*, was little observable beside the variety of Lamps, and frequent draughts of the holy Candlestick. In authentick draughts of *Anthony* and *Jerome*, we meet with thigh-bones and deaths heads; but the cemiteriall Cels of ancient Christians and Martyrs, were filled with draughts of Scripture Stories; not declining the flourishes of Cypresse, Palmes, and Olive; and the mysticall Figures of Peacocks, Doves and Cocks. But iterately affecting the pourtraits of *Enoch*, *Lazarus*, *Jonas*, and the Vision of *Ezechiel*, as hopefull draughts, and hinting imagery of the Resurrection; which is the life of the grave, and sweetens our habitations in the Land of Moles and Pismires.

Gentile Inscriptions precisely delivered the extent of mens lives, seldome the manner of their deaths, which history it self so often leaves obscure in the records of memorable persons. There is scarce any Philosopher but dies twice or thrice in *Laertius*; Nor almost any life without two or three deaths in *Plutarch*; which makes the tragicall ends of noble persons more favourably resented by compassionate Readers, who finde some relief in the Election of such differences.

The certainty of death is attended with uncertainties, in time, manner, places. The variety of Monuments hath often obscured true graves: and *Cenotaphs* confounded Sepulchres. For beside their reall Tombs, many have founded honorary and empty Sepulchres. The variety of *Homers* Monuments made him of various Countreys. *Euripides* had his Tomb in *Attica*, but his sepulture in *Macedonia*. And *Severus* found his real Sepulchre in *Rome*, but his empty grave in *Gallia*.

He that lay in a golden Urne eminently above the Earth, was not likely to finde the quiet of these bones. Many of these Urnes were broke by a vulgar discoverer in hope of inclosed treasure. The ashes of *Marcellus* were lost above ground, upon the like account. Where profit hath prompted, no age hath wanted such miners. For which the most barbarous Expilators found the most civill Rhetorick. Gold once out of the earth is no more due unto it; What was unreasonably committed to the ground is reasonably resumed from it: Let Monuments and rich Fabricks, not Riches adorn mens ashes. The commerce of the living is not to be transferred unto the dead: It is no injustice to take that which none complains to lose, and no man is wronged where no man is possessor.

What virtue yet sleeps in this *terra damnata* and aged cinders, were petty magick to experiment; These crumbling reliques and long-fired particles superannuate such expectations: Bones, hairs, nails, and teeth of the dead, were the treasures of old Sorcerers. In vain we revive such practices; Present superstition too visibly perpetuates the folly of our Fore-fathers, wherein unto old Observation this Island was so compleat, that it might have instructed *Persia*.

Plato's historian of the other world lies twelve dayes incorrupted, while his soul was viewing the large stations of the dead. How to keep the corps seven dayes from corruption by anointing and washing, without exenteration, were an hazardable peece of art, in our choisest practise. How they made distinct separation of bones and ashes from fiery admixture, hath found no historicall solution. Though they seemed to make a distinct collection, and overlooked not *Pyrrhus* his toe. Some provision they might make by fictile Vessels, Coverings, Tiles, or flat stones, upon and about the body. And in the same Field, not farre from these Urnes, many stones were found under ground, as also by carefull separation of extraneous matter, composing and raking up the burnt bones with forks, observable in that notable Lamp of *Galvanus. Marlianus*, who had the sight of the *Vas Ustrinum*, or vessell wherein they burnt the dead, found in the Esquiline Field at *Rome*, might have afforded clearer solution. But their insatisfaction herein begat that remarkable invention in the Funerall Pyres of some Princes, by incombustible sheets made with a texture of *Asbestos*, incremable flax, or Salamanders wool, which preserved their bones and ashes incommixed.

How the bulk of a man should sink into so few pounds of bones and ashes, may seem strange unto any who considers not its constitution, and how slender a masse will remain upon an open and urging fire of the carnall composition. Even bones themselves reduced into ashes, do abate a notable proportion. And consisting much of a volatile salt, when that is fired out, make a light kind of cinders. Although their bulk be disproportionable to their weight, when the heavy principle of Salt is fired out, and the Earth almost only remaineth; Observable in sallow, which makes more Ashes than Oake; and discovers the common fraud of selling Ashes by measure, and not by ponderation.

Some bones make best Skeletons, some bodies quick and speediest ashes: Who would expect a quick flame from Hydropicall *Heraclitus*? The poysoned Souldier when his Belly brake, put out two pyres in *Plutarch*. But in the plague of *Athens*, one private pyre served two or three Intruders; and the *Saracens* burnt in large heaps, by the King of *Castile*, shewed how little Fuell sufficeth. Though the Funerall pyre of *Patroclus* took up an hundred foot, a peece of an old boat burnt *Pompey*; And if the burthen of *Isaac* were sufficient for an holocaust, a man may carry his owne pyre.

From animals are drawn good burning lights, and good medicines against burning; Though the seminall humour seems of a contrary nature to fire, yet the body compleated proves a combustible lump, wherein fire findes flame even from bones, and some fuell almost from all parts. Though the Metropolis of humidity seems least disposed unto it, which might render the sculls of these Urnes lesse burned than other bones. But all flies or sinks before fire almost in all bodies: When the common ligament is dissolved, the attenuable parts ascend, the rest subside in coal, calx or ashes.

To burn the bones of the King of *Edom* for Lyme, seems no irrationall ferity; But to drink of the ashes of dead relations, a passionate prodigality. He that hath the ashes of his friend, hath an everlasting treasure: where fire taketh leave, corruption slowly enters; In bones well burnt, fire makes a wall against it self; experimented in copels, and tests of metals, which consist of such ingredients. What the Sun compoundeth, fire analyseth, not transmuteth. That devouring agent leaves almost allwayes a morsell for the Earth, whereof all things are but a colonie; and which, if time permits, the mother Element will have in their primitive masse again.

He that looks for Urnes and old sepulchrall reliques, must not seek them in the ruines of Temples; where no Religion anciently placed them. These were found in a Field, according to ancient custome, in noble or private buriall; the old practise of the *Canaanites*, the Family of *Abraham*, and the burying place of *Josua*, in the borders of his possessions; and also agreeable unto *Roman* prac- tice to bury by high-wayes, whereby their Monuments were under eye: Memorials of themselves, and *memento's* of mortality unto living passengers; whom the Epitaphs of great ones were fain to beg to stay and look upon them. A language though sometimes used, not so proper in Church-Inscriptions. The sensible Rhetorick of the dead, to exemplarity of good life, first admitted the bones of pious men and Martyrs within Church-wals; which in succeeding ages crept into promiscuous practise. While *Constantine* was peculiarly favoured to be admitted unto the Church Porch; and the first thus buried in *England* was in the dayes of *Cuthred*.

Christians dispute how their bodies should lye in the grave. In urnall enterrment they clearly escaped this Controversie: Though we decline the Religious consideration, yet in cemiteriall and narrower burying places, to avoid confusion and crosse position, a certain posture were to be admitted; Which even Pagan civility observed. The *Persians* lay North and South, The *Megarians* and *Phœnicians* placed their heads to the East: The *Athenians*, some think, towards the West, which Christians still retain. And *Beda* will have it to be the posture of our Saviour. That he was crucified with his face towards the West, we will not contend with tradition and probable account; but we applaud not the hand of the Painter, in exalting his Crosse so high above those on either side; since hereof we finde no authentick account in history, and even the crosses found by *Helena* pretend no such distinction from longitude or dimension.

To be knav'd out of our graves, to have our sculs made drinking-bowls, and our bones turned into Pipes, to delight and sport our Enemies, are Tragicall abominations, escaped in burning Burials.

Urnall enterrments, and burnt Reliques lye not in fear of worms, or to be an heritage for Serpents; In carnall sepulture, corruptions seem peculiar unto parts, and some speak of snakes out of the spinall marrow. But while we suppose common wormes in graves, 'tis not easie to finde any there; few in Church-yards above a foot deep, fewer or none in Churches, though in fresh decayed bodies. Teeth, bones, and hair, give the most lasting defiance to corruption. In an Hydropicall body ten years buried in a Church-yard, we met with a fat concretion, where the nitre of the Earth, and the salt and lixivious liquor of the body, had coagulated large lumps of fat, into the consistence of the hardest castle-soap; whereof part remaineth with us. After a battle with the *Persians* the *Roman* Corps decayed in few dayes, while the *Persian* bodies remained dry and uncorrupted. Bodies in the same ground do not uniformly dissolve, nor bones equally moulder; whereof in the opprobrious disease we expect no long duration. The body of the Marquesse of *Dorset* seemed sound and handsomely cereclothed, that after seventy eight years was found uncorrupted. Common Tombs preserve not beyond powder: A firmer consistence and compage of parts might be expected from Arefaction, deep buriall or charcoal. The greatest Antiquities of mortall bodies may remain in petrified bones, whereof, though we take not in the pillar of *Lots* wife, or Metamorphosis of *Ortelius*, some may be older than Pyramids, in the petrified Reliques of the generall inundation. When *Alexander* opened the Tomb of *Cyrus*, the remaining bones discovered his proportion, whereof urnall fragments afford but a bad conjecture, and have this disadvantage of grave enterrments, that they leave us ignorant of most personall discoveries. For since bones afford not only rectitude and stability, but figure unto the body; It is no impossible Physiognomy to conjecture at fleshy appendencies; and after what shape the muscles and carnous parts might hang in their full consistences.

A full spread *Cariola** shews a well-shaped horse behinde, handsome formed sculls give some analogie of fleshy resemblance. A criticall view of bones makes a good distinction of sexes. Even colour is not beyond conjecture; since it is hard to be deceived in the distinction of *Negro's* sculls. *Dantes* Characters are to be found in sculls as well as faces. *Hercules* is not onely known by his foot. Other parts make out their comproportions, and inferences upon whole or parts. And since the dimensions of the head measure the whole body, and the figure thereof gives conjecture of the principall faculties; Physiognomy outlives our selves, and ends not in our graves.

Severe contemplators observing these lasting reliques, may think them good monuments of persons past, little advantage to future beings. And considering that power which subdueth all things unto it self, that can resume the scattered Atomes, or identifie out of any thing, conceive it superfluous to expect a resurrection out of Reliques. But the soul subsisting, other matter clothed with due accidents may salve the individuality: Yet the Saints we observe arose from graves and monuments, about the holy City. Some think the ancient Patriarchs so earnestly desired to lay their bones in *Canaan*, as hoping to make a part of that Resurrection, and though thirty miles from Mount *Calvary*, at least to lie in that Region, which should produce the first-fruits of the dead. And if according to learned conjecture, the bodies of

* That part in the skeleton of an Horse, which is made by the hanch-bones

men shall rise where their greatest Reliques remain, many are not like to erre in the Topography of their Resurrection, though their bones or bodies be after translated by Angels into the field of *Ezechiels* vision, or as some will order it, into the Valley of Judgement, or *Jehosaphat*.

Chapter IV

Christians have handsomely glossed the deformity of death, by careful consideration of the body, and civil rites which take off brutall terminations. And though they conceived all reparable by a resurrection, cast not off all care of enterrment. For since the ashes of Sacrifices burnt upon the Altar of God, were carefully carried out by the Priests, and deposed in a clean field; since they acknowledged their bodies to be the lodging of Christ, and temples of the holy Ghost, they devolved not all upon the sufficiency of soul existence; and therefore with long services and full solemnities concluded their last Exequies, wherein to all distinctions the Greek devotion seems most pathetically ceremonious.

Christian invention hath chiefly driven at Rites, which speak hopes of another life, and hints of a Resurrection. And if the ancient Gentiles held not the immortality of their better part, and some subsistence after death; in severall rites, customes, actions and expressions, they contradicted their own opinions: wherein *Democritus* went high, even to the thought of a resurrection, as scoffingly recorded by *Pliny*. What can be more expresse than the expression of *Phocyllides*? Or who would expect from *Lucretius* a sentence of *Ecclesiastes*? Before *Plato* could speak, the soul had wings in *Homer*, which fell not, but flew out of the body into the mansions of the dead; who also observed that handsome distinction of *Demas* and *Soma*, for the body conjoyned to the soul and body separated from it. *Lucian* spoke much truth in jest, when he said, that part of *Hercules* which proceeded from *Alchmena* perished, that from *Jupiter* remained immortall. Thus *Socrates* was content that his friends should bury his body, so they would not think they buried *Socrates*, and regarding only his immortall part, was indifferent to be burnt or buried. From such Considerations *Diogenes* might contemn Sepulture. And being satisfied that the soul could not perish, grow carelesse of corporall enterrment. The *Stoicks* who thought the souls of wise men had their habitation about the *moon*, might make slight account of subterraneous deposition; whereas the *Pythagorians* and transcorporating Philosophers, who were to be often buried, held great care of their enterrment. And the Platonicks rejected not a due care of the grave, though they put their ashes to unreasonable expectations, in their tedious term of return and long set revolution.

Men have lost their reason in nothing so much as their religion, wherein stones and clouts make Martyrs; and since the religion of one seems madnesse unto another, to afford an account or rationall of old Rites, requires no rigid Reader; That they kindled the pyre aversly, or turning their face from it, was an handsome Symbole of unwilling ministration; That they washed their bones with wine and milk, that the mother wrapt them in Linnen, and dryed them in her bosome, the first fostering part, and place of their nourishment; That they opened their eyes towards heaven, before they kindled the fire, as the place of their hopes or originall, were no improper Ceremonies. Their last valediction thrice uttered by the attendants was also very solemn, and somewhat answered by Christians, who thought it too little, if they threw not the earth thrice upon the enterred body. That in strewing their Tombs the *Romans* affected the Rose, the Greeks *Amaranthus* and myrtle; that the Funerall pyre consisted of sweet fuell, Cypresse, Firre, Larix, Yewe, and Trees perpetually verdant, lay silent expressions of their surviving hopes: Wherein Christians which deck their Coffins with Bays have found a more elegant Embleme. For that tree seeming dead, will restore it self from the root, and its dry and exuccous leaves resume their verdure again; which if we mistake not, we have also observed in furze. Whether the planting of yewe in Churchyards hold not its originall from ancient Funerall rites, or as an Embleme of Resurrection from its perpetual verdure, may also admit conjecture.

They made use of Musick to excite or quiet the affections of their friends, according to different harmonies. But the secret and symbolicall hint was the harmonical nature of the soul; which delivered from the body, went again to enjoy the primitive harmony of heaven, from whence it first descended; which according to its progresse traced by antiquity, came down by *Cancer*, and ascended by *Capricornus*.

They burnt not children before their teeth appeared,

as apprehending their bodies too tender a morsell for fire, and that their gristly bones would scarce leave separable reliques after the pyrall combustion. That they kindled not fire in their houses for some dayes after, was a strict memoriall of the late afflicting fire. And mourning without hope, they had an happy fraud against excessive lamentation, by a common opinion that deep sorrows disturbed their ghosts.

That they buried their dead on their backs, or in a supine position, seems agreeable unto profound sleep, and common posture of dying; contrary to the most naturall way of birth; nor like our pendulous posture, in the doubtfull state of the womb. *Diogenes* was singular, who preferred a prone situation in the grave, and some Christians like neither, who decline the figure of rest, and make choice of an erect posture.

That they carried them out of the world with their feet forward, not inconsonant unto reason: As contrary unto the native posture of man, and his production first into it. And also agreeable unto their opinions, while they bid adieu unto the world, not to look again upon it; whereas *Mahometans* who think to return to a delight-full life again, are carried forth with their heads forward, and looking toward their houses.

They closed their eyes as parts which first die or first discover the sad effects of death. But their iterated clamations to excite their dying or dead friends, or revoke them unto life again, was a vanity of affection; as not presumably ignorant of the criticall tests of death, by apposition of feathers, glasses, and reflexion of figures, which dead eyes represent not; which however not strictly verifiable in fresh and warm *cadavers*, could hardly elude the test, in corps of four or five dayes.

That they suck'd in the last breath of their expiring friends, was surely a practice of no medicall institution, but a loose opinion that the soul passed out that way, and a fondnesse of affection from some *Pythagoricall* foundation, that the spirit of one body passed into another; which they wished might be their own.

That they powred oyle upon the pyre, was a tolerable practise, while the intention rested in facilitating the accension; But to place good *Omens* in the quick and speedy burning, to sacrifice unto the windes for a dispatch in this office, was a low form of superstition.

The *Archimime* or *Jester* attending the Funerall train, and imitating the speeches, gesture, and manners of the deceased, was too light for such solemnities, contradicting their Funerall Orations, and dolefull rites of the grave.

That they buried a peece of money with them as a Fee of the *Elysian Ferry-man*, was a practise full of folly. But the ancient custome of placing coynes in considerable Urnes, and the present practise of burying medals in the Noble Foundations of *Europe*, are laudable wayes of historicall discoveries, in actions, persons, Chronologies; and posterity will applaud them.

We examine not the old Laws of Sepulture, exempting certain persons from buriall or burning. But hereby we apprehend that these were not the bones of persons Planet-struck or burnt with fire from Heaven: No Reliques of Traitors to their Countrey, Self-killers, or Sacrilegious Malefactors; Persons in old apprehension unworthy of the *earth*; condemned unto the *Tartarus* of Hell, and bottomlesse pit of *Pluto*, from whence there was no redemption.

Nor were only many customes questionable in order to their Obsequies, but also sundry practises, fictions, and conceptions, discordant or obscure, of their state and future beings; whether unto eight or ten bodies of men to adde one of a woman, as being more inflammable, and unctuously constituted for the better pyrall combustion, were any rationall practise: Or whether the complaint of *Perianders* Wife be tolerable, that wanting her Funerall burning she suffered intolerable cold in Hell, according to the constitution of the infernall house of *Pluto*, wherein cold makes a great part of their tortures; it cannot passe without some question.

Why the Female Ghosts appear unto *Ulysses*, before the *Heroes* and masculine spirits? Why the *Psyche* or soul of *Tiresias* is of the masculine gender; who being blinde on earth sees more than all the rest in hell; Why the Funerall Suppers consisted of Egges, Beans, Smallage, and Lettuce, since the dead are made to eat *Asphodels* about the *Elyzian* medows? Why since there is no Sacrifice acceptable, nor any propitiation for the Covenant of the grave; men set up the Deity of *Morta*, and fruitlessly adored Divinities without ears? it cannot escape some doubt.

The dead seem all alive in the human *Hades* of *Homer*, yet cannot well speak, prophesie, or know the living, except they drink bloud, wherein is the life of man. And therefore the souls of *Penelope's* Paramours conducted by *Mercury* chirped like bats, and those which followed *Hercules* made a noise but like a flock of birds.

The departed spirits know things past and to come, yet are ignorant of things present. *Agamemnon* foretels what should happen unto *Ulysses*, yet ignorantly enquires what is become of his own Son. The Ghosts are afraid of swords in *Homer*, yet *Sybilla* tels *Æneas* in *Virgil*, the thin habit of spirits was beyond the force of weapons. The spirits put off their malice with their bodies, and *Cæsar* and *Pompey* accord in Latine Hell, yet *Ajax* in *Homer* endures not a conference with *Ulysses*: And *Deiphobus* appears all mangled in *Virgils* Ghosts, yet we meet with perfect shadows among the wounded ghosts of *Homer*.

Since *Charon* in *Lucian* applauds his condition among the dead, whether it be handsomely said of *Achilles*, that living contemner of death, that he had rather be a Plowmans servant than Emperour of the dead? How *Hercules* his soul is in hell, and yet in heaven, and *Julius* his soul in a Starre, yet seen by *Æneas* in hell, except the Ghosts were but Images and shadows of the soul, received in higher mansions, according to the ancient division of body, soul, and image or *simulachrum* of them both. The particulars of future beings must needs be dark unto ancient Theories, which Christian Philosophy yet determines but in a Cloud of opinions. A Dialogue between two Infants in the womb concerning the state of this world, might handsomely illustrate our ignorance of the next, whereof methinks we yet discourse in *Platoes* denne, and are but *Embryon* Philosophers.

Pythagoras escapes in the fabulous hell of *Dante*, among that swarm of Philosophers, wherein whilest we meet with *Plato* and *Socrates*, *Cato* is to be found in no lower place than Purgatory. Among all the set, *Epicurus* is most considerable, whom men make honest without an *Elyzium*, who contemned life without encouragement of immortality, and making nothing after death, yet made nothing of the King of terrours.

Were the happinesse of the next world as closely apprehended as the felicities of this, it were a martyr-dome to live; and unto such as consider none hereafter, it must be more than death to dye, which makes us amazed at those audacities, that durst be nothing, and return into their *Chaos* again. Certainly such spirits as could contemn death, when they expected no better being after, would have scorned to live had they known any. And therefore we applaud not the judgment of *Machiavel*, that Christianity makes men cowards, or that with the confidence of but half dying, the despised virtues of patience and humility have abased the spirits of men, which Pagan principles exalted, but rather regulated the wildenesse of audacities, in the attempts, grounds, and eternall sequels of death; wherein men of the boldest spirits are often prodigiously temerarious. Nor can we extenuate the valour of ancient Martyrs, who contemned death in the uncomfortable scene of their lives, and in their decrepit Martyrdomes did probably lose not many moneths of their dayes, or parted with life when it was scarce worth the living. For (beside that long time past holds no consideration unto a slender time to come) they had no small disadvantage from the constitution of old age, which naturally makes men fearfull; com-plexionally superannuated from the bold and couragious thoughts of youth and fervent years. But the contempt of death from corporall animosity promoteth not our felicity. They may sit in the *Orchestra*, and noblest Seats of Heaven, who have held up shaking hands in the fire, and humanly contended for glory.

Mean while *Epicurus* lyes deep in *Dante's* hell, wherein we meet with Tombs enclosing souls which denied their immortalities. But whether the virtuous heathen, who lived better than he spake, or erring in the principles of himself, yet lived above Philosophers of more specious Maximes, lye so deep as he is placed; at least so low as not to rise against Christians, who beleeving or knowing that truth, have lastingly denied it in their practise and conversation, were a quæry too sad to insist on.

But all or most apprehensions rested in Opinions of some future being, which ignorantly or coldly beleeved, begat those perverted conceptions, Ceremonies, Sayings, which Christians pity or laugh at. Happy are they, which live not in that disadvantage of time, when men could say little for futurity, but from reason. Whereby the noblest mindes fell often upon doubtfull deaths, and melancholly Dissolutions; With these hopes *Socrates* warmed his doubtfull spirits against that cold potion, and *Cato* before he durst give the fatall stroak spent part of the night in reading the immortality of *Plato*, thereby confirming his wavering hand unto the animosity of that attempt.

It is the heaviest stone that melancholy can throw at a man, to tell him he is at the end of his nature; or that there is no further state to come, unto which this seemes progressionall, and otherwise made in vaine; Without this accomplishment the naturall expectation and desire of such a state, were but a fallacy in nature; unsatisfied Considerators would quarrell the justice of their constitutions, and rest content that *Adam* had fallen lower, whereby by knowing no other Originall, and deeper ignorance of themselves, they might have enjoyed the happinesse of inferiour Creatures; who in tranquility possesse their Constitutions, as having not the apprehension to deplore their own natures. And being framed below the circumference of these hopes, or cognition of better being, the wisedom of God hath necessitated their Contentment: But the superiour ingredient and obscured part of our selves, whereto all present felicities afford no resting contentment, will be able at last to tell us we are more than our present selves; and evacuate such hopes in the fruition of their own accomplishments.

Chapter V

Now since these dead bones have already out-lasted the living ones of *Methuselah*, and in a yard under ground, and thin walls of clay, out-worn all the strong and specious buildings above it; and quietly rested under the drums and tramplings of three conquests; What Prince can promise such diuturnity unto his Reliques, or might not gladly say,

Sic ego componi versus in ossa velim.*

Time which antiquates Antiquities, and hath an art to make dust of all things, hath yet spared these *minor*

* Thus, when naught is left of me but bones, would I be laid to rest.

Monuments. In vain we hope to be known by open and visible conservatories, when to be unknown was the means of their continuation and obscurity their protection: If they dyed by violent hands, and were thrust into their Urnes, these bones become considerable, and some old Philosophers would honour them, whose souls they conceived most pure, which were thus snatched from their bodies; and to retain a stronger propension unto them: whereas they weariedly left a languishing corps, and with faint desires of re-union. If they fell by long and aged decay, yet wrapt up in the bundle of time, they fall into indistinction, and make but one blot with Infants. If we begin to die when we live, and long life be but a prolongation of death, our life is a sad composition; We live with death, and die not in a moment. How many pulses made up the life of *Methuselah*, were work for *Archimedes*: Common Counters summe up the life of *Moses* his man. Our dayes become considerable like petty sums by minute accumulations; where numerous fractions make up but small round numbers; and our dayes of a span long make not one little finger.

If the nearnesse of our last necessity brought a nearer conformity unto it, there were a happinesse in hoary hairs, and no calamity in half senses. But the long habit of living indisposeth us for dying; When Avarice makes us the sport of death; When even *David* grew politickly cruell; and *Solomon* could hardly be said to be the wisest of men. But many are too early old, and before the date of age. Adversity stretcheth our dayes, misery makes *Alcmenas* nights,*

* One night as long as three.

and time hath no wings unto it. But the most tedious being is that which can unwish it self, content to be nothing, or never to have been, which was beyond the *male*-content of *Job*, who cursed not the day of his life, but his Nativity: Content to have so farre been, as to have a Title to future being; Although he had lived here but in an hidden state of life, and as it were an abortion.

What Song the *Syrens* sang, or what name *Achilles* assumed when he hid himself among women, though puzling Questions are not beyond all conjecture. What time the persons of these Ossuaries entred the famous Nations of the dead, and slept with Princes and Coun-sellours, might admit a wide solution. But who were the proprietaries of these bones, or what bodies these ashes made up, were a question above Antiquarism. Not to be resolved by man, nor easily perhaps by spirits, except we consult the Provinciall Guardians, or tutellary Observa-tors. Had they made as good provision for their names, as they have done for their Reliques, they had not so grosly erred in the art of perpetuation. But to subsist in bones, and be but Pyramidally extant, is a fallacy in duration. Vain ashes, which in the oblivion of names, persons, times, and sexes, have found unto themselves a fruitlesse continuation, and only arise unto late posterity, as Emblemes of mortall vanities; Antidotes against pride, vainglory, and madding vices. Pagan vain-glories which thought the world might last for ever, had encourage-ment for ambition, and finding no *Atropos* unto the immortality of their Names, were never dampt with the necessity of oblivion. Even old ambitions had the advantage of ours, in the attempts of their vainglories, who acting early, and before the probable Meridian of time, have by this time found great accomplishment of their designes, whereby the ancient *Heroes* have already out-lasted their Monuments, and Mechanicall preservations. But in this latter Scene of time we cannot expect such Mummies unto our memories, when ambition may fear the Prophecy of *Elias*, and *Charles* the fifth can never hope to live within two *Methusela's* of *Hector*.*

And therefore restlesse inquietude for the diuturnity of our memories unto present considerations seems a vanity almost out of date, and superanuated peece of folly. We cannot hope to live so long in our names as some have done in their persons, one face of *Janus* holds no proportion unto the other. 'Tis too late to be ambitious. The great mutations of the world are acted, our time may be too short for our designes. To extend our memories by Monuments, whose death we dayly pray for, and whose duration we cannot hope, without injury to our expectations in the advent of the last day, were a contradiction to our beliefs. We whose generations are ordained in this setting part of time, are providentially taken off from such imaginations. And being necessitated to eye the remaining particle of futurity, are naturally constituted unto thoughts of the next world, and cannot excusably decline the consideration of that duration, which maketh Pyramids pillars of snow, and all that's past a moment.

Circles and right lines limit and close all bodies, and

---

* Hector's fame lasting above two lives of Methuselah, before that famous Prince was extant.

the mortall right-lined circle* must conclude and shut up all. There is no antidote against the *Opium* of time, which temporally considereth all things; Our Fathers finde their graves in our short memories, and sadly tell us how we may be buried in our Survivors. Grave-stones tell truth scarce fourty years: Generations passe while some trees stand, and old Families last not three Oaks. To be read by bare Inscriptions like many in *Gruter*, to hope for Eternity by Ænigmaticall Epithetes, or first letters of our names, to be studied by Antiquaries, who we were, and have new Names given us like many of the Mummies, are cold consolations unto the Students of perpetuity, even by everlasting Languages.

To be content that times to come should only know there was such a man, not caring whether they knew more of him, was a frigid ambition in *Cardan.* disparaging his horoscopal inclination and judgement of himself. Who cares to subsist like *Hippocrates* Patients, or *Achilles* horses in *Homer*, under naked nominations, without deserts and noble acts, which are the balsame of our memories, the *Entelechia* and soul of our subsistences? To be namelesse in worthy deeds exceeds an infamous history. The *Canaanitish* woman lives more happily without a name, than *Herodias* with one. And who had not rather have been the good theef, than *Pilate*?

But the iniquity of oblivion blindely scattereth her poppy, and deals with the memory of men without distinction to merit of perpetuity. Who can but pity the founder of the Pyramids? *Herostratus* lives that burnt the

---

* θ The Character of death.

Temple of *Diana*, he is almost lost that built it; Time hath spared the Epitaph of *Adrians* horse, confounded that of himself. In vain we compute our felicities by the advantage of our good names, since bad have equall durations; and *Thersites* is like to live as long as *Agamemnon*. Who knows whether the best of men be known? or whether there be not more remarkable persons forgot, than any that stand remembred in the known account of time? Without the favour of the everlasting Register the first man had been as unknown as the last, and *Methuselahs* long life had been his only Chronicle.

Oblivion is not to be hired: The greater part must be content to be as though they had not been, to be found in the Register of God, not in the record of man. Twenty seven Names make up the first story,* and the recorded names ever since contain not one living Century. The number of the dead long exceedeth all that shall live. The night of time far surpasseth the day, and who knows when was the Æquinox? Every houre addes unto that current Arithmetique, which scarce stands one moment. And since death must be the *Lucina* of life, and even Pagans could doubt whether thus to live, were to dye. Since our longest Sunne sets at right descensions, and makes but winter arches, and therefore it cannot be long before we lie down in darknesse, and have our light in ashes.† Since the brother of death daily haunts us with dying *memento's*, and time that grows old it self, bids us

---

* Before the flood.

† According to the custome of the Jewes, who place a lighted wax-candle in a pot of ashes by the corps.

hope no long duration: Diuturnity is a dream and folly of expectation.

Darknesse and light divide the course of time, and oblivion shares with memory a great part even of our living beings; we slightly remember our felicities, and the smartest stroaks of affliction leave but short smart upon us. Sense endureth no extremities, and sorrows destroy us or themselves. To weep into stones are fables. Afflictions induce callosities, miseries are slippery, or fall like snow upon us, which notwithstanding is no unhappy stupidity. To be ignorant of evils to come, and forgetfull of evils past, is a mercifull provision in nature, whereby we digest the mixture of our few and evil dayes, and our delivered senses not relapsing into cutting remembrances, our sorrows are not kept raw by the edge of repetitions. A great part of Antiquity contented their hopes of subsistency with a transmigration of their souls. A good way to continue their memories, while having the advantage of plurall successions, they could not but act something remarkable in such variety of beings, and enjoying the fame of their passed selves, make accumulation of glory unto their last durations. Others rather than be lost in the uncomfortable night of nothing, were content to recede into the common being, and make one particle of the publick soul of all things, which was no more than to return into their unknown and divine Originall again. Ægyptian ingenuity was more unsatisfied, continuing their bodies in sweet consistences, to attend the return of their souls. But all was vanity, feeding the winde, and folly. The Ægyptian Mummies, which *Cambyses* or time hath spared, avarice now consumeth. Mummie is become Merchandise, *Miszraim* cures wounds, and *Pharaob* is sold for balsoms.

In vain do individuals hope for Immortality, or any patent from oblivion, in preservations below the Moon: Men have been deceived even in their flatteries above the Sun, and studied conceits to perpetuate their names in heaven. The various Cosmography of that part hath already varied the names of contrived constellations; *Nimrod* is lost in *Orion*, and *Osyris* in the Dogge-starre. While we look for incorruption in the heavens, we finde they are but like the Earth; Durable in their main bodies, alterable in their parts: whereof beside Comets and new Stars, perspectives begin to tell tales. And the spots that wander about the Sun, with *Phaetons* favour, would make clear conviction.

There is nothing strictly immortall, but immortality. Whatever hath no beginning may be confident of no end (all others have a dependent being, and within the reach of destruction) which is the peculiar of that necessary essence that cannot destroy it self; And the highest strain of omnipotency to be so powerfully constituted, as not to suffer even from the power of it self. But the sufficiency of Christian Immortality frustrates all earthly glory, and the quality of either state after death makes a folly of posthumous memory. God who only can destroy our souls, and hath assured our resurrection, either of our bodies or names hath directly promised no duration. Wherein there is so much of chance that the boldest Expectants have found unhappy frustration; and to hold long subsistence, seems but a scape in oblivion. But man is a Noble Animal, splendid in ashes, and pompous in the grave, solemnizing Nativities and Deaths with equall lustre, nor omitting Ceremonies of bravery, in the infamy of his nature.

Life is a pure flame, and we live by an invisible Sun within us. A small fire sufficeth for life, great flames seemed too little after death, while men vainly affected precious pyres, and to burn like *Sardanapalus*; but the wisedom of funerall Laws found the folly of prodigall blazes, and reduced undoing fires unto the rule of sober obsequies, wherein few could be so mean as not to provide wood, pitch, a mourner, and an Urne.

Five languages secured not the Epitaph of *Gordianus*; The man of God lives longer without a Tomb than any by one, invisibly interred by Angels, and adjudged to obscurity though not without some marks directing human discovery. *Enoch* and *Elias* without either tomb or buriall, in an anomalous state of being, are the great Examples of perpetuity in their long and living memory, in strict account being still on this side death, and having a late part yet to act upon this stage of earth. If in the decretory term of the world we shall not all dye but be changed, according to received translation, the last day will make but few graves; at least quick Resurrections will anticipate lasting Sepultures; Some Graves will be opened before they be quite closed, and *Lazarus* be no wonder. When many that feared to dye shall groane that they can dye but once, the dismall state is the second and living death; when life puts despair on the damned; when men shall wish the coverings of Mountaines, not of Monuments, and annihilation shall be courted.

While some have studied Monuments, others have

studiously declined them: and some have been so vainly boisterous, that they durst not acknowledge their Graves; wherein *Alaricus* seems most subtle, who had a River turned to hide his bones at the bottome. Even *Sylla* that thought himself safe in his Urne, could not prevent revenging tongues, and stones thrown at his Monument. Happy are they whom privacy makes innocent, who deal so with men in this world, that they are not afraid to meet them in the next, who when they dye, make no commotion among the dead, and are not toucht with that poeticall taunt of *Isaiah*.

. *Pyramids, Arches, Obelisks*, were but the irregularities of vainglory, and wilde enormities of ancient magnanimity. But the most magnanimous resolution rests in the Christian Religion, which trampleth upon pride, and sits on the neck of ambition, humbly pursuing that infallible perpetuity, unto which all others must diminish their diameters, and be poorly seen in Angles of contingency.*

Pious spirits who passed their dayes in raptures of futurity, made little more of this world than the world that was before it, while they lay obscure in the Chaos of pre-ordination, and night of their fore-beings. And if any have been so happy as truly to understand Christian annihilation, extasis, exolution, liquefaction, transformation, the kisse of the Spouse, gustation of God, and ingression into the divine shadow, they have already had an handsome anticipation of heaven; the glory of the world is surely over, and the earth in ashes unto them.

To subsist in lasting Monuments, to live in their

* *Angulas contingentiae*, the least of Angles.

productions, to exist in their names, and prædicament of *Chymera's*, was large satisfaction unto old expectations, and made one part of their *Elyziums*. But all this is nothing in the Metaphysicks of true belief. To live indeed is to be again our selves, which being not only an hope but an evidence in noble beleevers, 'Tis all one to lye in St *Innocents*★ Church-yard, as in the Sands of *Ægypt*: Ready to be any thing, in the extasie of being ever, and as content with six foot as the Moles of *Adrianus*.†

> *Lucan*
> —Tabesne cadavera solvat
> An rogus haud refert.‡—

★ In Paris where bodies soon consume.
† A stately *Mausoleum* or sepulchral pyle built by Adrianus in Rome, where now standeth the Castle of St. Angelo.
‡ It matters not whether the corpses are burnt on the pyre or decompose with time.

A Letter to a Friend, Upon Occasion of the Death of his Intimate Friend

Give me leave to wonder that News of this nature should have such heavy Wings, that you should hear so little concerning your dearest Friend, and that I must make that unwilling Repetition to tell you,

Ad portam rigidos calces extendit,*

that he is Dead and Buried, and by this time no Puny among the mighty Nations of the Dead; for tho he left this World not very many days past, yet every hour you know largely addeth unto that dark Society; and considering the incessant Mortality of Mankind, you cannot conceive there dieth in the whole Earth so few as a thousand an hour.

Altho at this distance you had no early Account or Particular of his Death; yet your Affection may cease to wonder that you had not some secret Sense or Intimation thereof by Dreams, thoughtful Whisperings, Mercurisms, Airy Nuncio's, or sympathetical Insinuations, which many seem to have had at the Death of their dearest Friends: for since we find in that famous Story,

* He stretches out his heels cold and stark towards the door.

that Spirits themselves were fain to tell their Fellows at a distance, that the great *Antonio* was dead; we have a sufficient Excuse for our Ignorance in such Particulars, and must rest content with the common Road, and *Appian* way of Knowledge by Information. Tho the uncertainty of the End of this World hath confounded all Humane Predictions; yet they who shall live to see the Sun and Moon darkned, and the Stars to fall from Heaven, will hardly be deceived in the Advent of the last Day; and therefore strange it is, that the common Fallacy of consumptive Persons, who feel not themselves dying, and therefore still hope to live, should also reach their Friends in perfect Health and Judgment. That you should be so little acquainted with *Plautus's* sick Complexion, or that almost an *Hippocratical* Face should not alarum you to higher fears, or rather despair of his Continuation in such an emaciated State, wherein medical Predictions fail not, as sometimes in acute Diseases, and wherein 'tis as dangerous to be sentenced by a Physician as a Judge.

Upon my first Visit I was bold to tell them who had not let fall all hopes of his Recovery, That in my sad Opinion he was not like to behold a Grashopper, much less to pluck another Fig; and in no long time after seemed to discover that odd mortal Symptom in him not mention'd by *Hippocrates*, that is, to lose his own Face and look like some of his near Relations; for he maintained not his proper Countenance, but looked like his Uncle, the Lines of whose Face lay deep and invisible in his healthful Visage before: for as from our beginning we run through variety of Looks, before we come to consistent and settled Faces; so before our End, by sick and languishing Alterations, we put on new Visages: and in our Retreat to Earth, may fall upon such Looks which from community of seminal Originals were before latent in us.

He was fruitlessly put in hope of advantage by change of Air, and imbibing the pure Aerial Nitre of these Parts; and therefore being so far spent, he quickly found *Sardinia* in *Tivoli*, and the most healthful Air of little effect, where Death had set her Broad Arrow; for he lived not unto the middle of *May*, and confirmed the Observation of *Hippocrates* of that mortal time of the Year when the Leaves of the Fig-tree resemble a Daw's Claw. He is happily seated who lives in Places whose Air, Earth, and Water, promote not the Infirmities of his weaker Parts, or is early removed into Regions that correct them. He that is tabidly inclined, were unwise to pass his days in *Portugal:* Cholical Persons will find little Comfort in *Austria* or *Vienna*: He that is Weak-legg'd must not be in Love with *Rome*, nor an infirm Head with *Venice* or *Paris*. Death hath not only particular Stars in heaven, but malevolent Places on Earth, which single out our Infirmities, and strike at our weaker Parts; in which Concern, passager and migrant Birds have the great Advantages; who are naturally constituted for distant Habitations, whom no Seas nor Places limit, but in their appointed Seasons will visit us from *Greenland* and Mount *Atlas*, and as some think, even from the *Antipodes*.

Tho we could not have his Life, yet we missed not our desires in his soft Departure, which was scarce an Expiration; and his End not unlike his Beginning, when the salient Point scarce affords a sensible motion, and his

Departure so like unto Sleep, that he scarce needed the civil Ceremony of closing his Eyes; contrary unto the common way wherein Death draws up, Sleep lets fall the Eye-lids. With what strift and pains we came into the World we know not; but 'tis commonly no easie matter to get out of it: yet if it could be made out, that such who have easie Nativities have commonly hard Deaths, and contrarily; his Departure was so easie, that we might justly suspect his Birth was of another nature, and that some *Juno* sat cross-legg'd at his Nativity.

Besides his soft Death, the incurable state of his Disease might somewhat extenuate your Sorrow, who know that Monsters but seldom happen, Miracles more rarely, in Physick. *Angelus Victorius* gives a serious Account of a Consumptive, Hectical, Pthysical Woman, who was suddenly cured by the Intercession of *Ignatius*. We read not of any in Scripture who in this case applied unto our Saviour, tho some may be contained in that large Expression, That *he went about Galilee healing all manner of Sickness, and all manner of Diseases*. Amulets, Spells, Sigils and Incantations, practised in other Diseases, are seldom pretended in this; and we find no Sigil in the Archidoxis of *Paracelsus* to cure an extreme Consumption or *Marasmus*, which if other Diseases fail, will put a period unto long Livers, and at last make dust of all. And therefore the *Stoicks* could not but think that the firy Principle would wear out all the rest, and at last make an end of the World, which notwithstanding without such a lingring period the Creator may effect at his Pleasure: and to make an end of all things on Earth, and our Planetical System of the World, he need but put out the Sun.

I was not so curious to entitle the Stars unto any concern of his Death, yet could not but take notice that he died when the Moon was in motion from the Meridian; at which time, an old *Italian* long ago would persuade me, that the greatest part of Men died: but herein I confess I could never satisfie my Curiosity; altho from the time of Tides in Places upon or near the Sea, there may be considerable Deductions; and *Pliny* hath an odd and remarkable Passage concerning the Death of Men and Animals upon the Recess or Ebb of the Sea. However, certain it is he died in the dead and deep part of the Night, when *Nox* might be most apprehensibly said to be the Daughter of Chaos, the Mother of Sleep and Death, according to old Genealogy; and so went out of this World about that hour when our blessed Saviour entred it, and about what time many conceive he will return again unto it. *Cardan* hath a peculiar and no hard Observation from a Man's Hand, to know whether he was born in the day or night, which I confess holdeth in my own. And *Scaliger* to that purpose hath another from the tip of the Ear. Most Men are begotten in the Night, most Animals in the Day; but whether more Persons have been born in the Night or the Day, were a Curiosity undecidable, tho more have perished by violent Deaths in the Day; yet in natural Dissolutions both Times may hold an Indifferency, at least but contingent Inequality. The whole course of Time runs out in the Nativity and Death of Things; which whether they happen by

Succession or Coincidence, are best computed by the natural, not artificial Day.

That *Charles* the Fifth was Crowned upon the day of his Nativity, it being in his own power so to order it, makes no singular Animadversion; but that he should also take King *Francis* Prisoner upon that day, was an unexpected Coincidence, which made the same remarkable. *Antipater* who had an Anniversary Fever every Year upon his Birth day, needed no Astrological Revolution to know what day he should dye on. When the fixed Stars have made a Revolution unto the points from whence they first set out, some of the Ancients thought the World would have an end; which was a kind of dying upon the day of its Nativity. Now the Disease prevailing and swiftly advancing about the time of his Nativity, some were of Opinion, that he would leave the World on the day he entered into it: but this being a lingring Disease, and creeping softly on, nothing critical was found or expected, and he died not before fifteen days after. Nothing is more common with Infants than to dye on the day of their Nativity, to behold the worldly Hours and but the Fractions thereof; and even to perish before their Nativity in the hidden World of the Womb, and before their good Angel is conceived to undertake them. But in Persons who out-live many Years, and when there are no less than three hundred sixty five days to determine their Lives in every Year; that the first day should make the last, that the Tail of the Snake should return into its Mouth precisely at that time, and they should wind up upon the day of their Nativity, is indeed a remarkable Coincidence, which tho Astrology hath taken witty pains to salve, yet hath it been very wary in making Predictions of it.

In this consumptive Condition and remarkable Extenuation he came to be almost half himself, and left a great part behind him which he carried not to the Grave. And tho that Story of Duke *John Ernestus Mansfield* be not so easily swallowed, that at his Death his Heart was found not to be so big as a Nut; yet if the Bones of a good Sceleton weigh little more than twenty pounds, his Inwards and Flesh remaining could make no Bouff-age, but a light bit for the Grave. I never more lively beheld the starved Characters of *Dante* in any living Face; an Aruspex might have read a Lecture upon him without Exenteration, his Flesh being so consumed that he might, in a manner, have discerned his Bowels without opening of him: so that to be carried *sextâ cervice* to the Grave, was but a civil unnecessity; and the Complements of the Coffin might out-weigh the Subject of it.

Omnibonus Ferrarius in mortal Dysenteries of Children looks for a Spot behind the Ear; in consumptive Diseases some eye the Complexion of Moals; *Cardan* eagerly views the Nails, some the Lines of the Hand, the Thenar or Muscle of the Thumb; some are so curious as to observe the depth of the Throat-pit, how the proportion varieth of the Small of the Legs unto the Calf, or the compass of the Neck unto the Circumference of the Head: but all these, with many more, were so drowned in a mortal Visage and last Face of *Hippocrates*, that a weak Physiognomist might say at first eye, This was a Face of Earth, and that *Morta* had set her Hard-Seal upon his Temples, easily perceiving what *Caricatura* Draughts

Death makes upon pined Faces, and unto what an unknown degree a Man may live backward.

Tho the Beard be only made a distinction of Sex and sign of masculine Heat by *Ulmus*, yet the Precocity and early growth thereof in him, was not to be liked in reference unto long Life. *Lewis*, that virtuous but unfortunate King of *Hungary*, who lost his Life at the Battel of *Mohacz*, was said to be born without a Skin, to have bearded at Fifteen, and to have shewn some gray Hairs about Twenty; from whence the Diviners conjectured, that he would be spoiled of his Kingdom, and have but a short Life: But Hairs make fallible Predictions, and many Temples early gray have out-lived the Psalmist's Period. Hairs which have most amused me have not been in the Face or Head but on the Back, and not in Men but Children, as I long ago observed in that Endemial Distemper of little Children in *Languedock*, called the *Morgellons*, wherein they critically break out with harsh Hairs on their Backs, which takes off the unquiet Symptoms of the Disease, and delivers them from Coughs and Convulsions.

The *Egyptian* Mummies that I have seen, have had their Mouths open, and somewhat gaping, which affordeth a good opportunity to view and observe their Teeth, wherein 'tis not easie to find any wanting or decayed: and therefore in *Egypt*, where one Man practised but one Operation, or the Diseases but of single Parts, it must needs be a barren Profession to confine unto that of drawing of Teeth, and little better than to have been Tooth-drawer unto King *Pyrrbus*, who had but two in his Head. How the *Bannyans* of *India* maintain the Integrity of those Parts, I find not particularly observed; who notwithstanding have an Advantage of their Preservation by abstaining from all Flesh, and employing their Teeth in such Food unto which they may seem at first framed, from their Figure and Conformation: but sharp and corroding Rheums had so early mouldred those Rocks and hardest parts of his Fabrick, that a Man might well conceive that his Years were never like to double or twice tell over his Teeth. Corruption had dealt more severely with them, than sepulchral Fires and smart Flames with those of burnt Bodies of old; for in the burnt Fragments of Urns which I have enquired into, altho I seem to find few Incisors or Shearers, yet the Dog Teeth and Grinders do notably resist those Fires.

In the Years of his Childhood he had languished under the Disease of his Country, the Rickets; after which notwithstanding many I have seen become strong and active Men; but whether any have attained unto very great Years the Disease is scarce so old as to afford good Observation. Whether the Children of the *English* Plantations be subject unto the same Infirmity, may be worth the observing. Whether Lameness and Halting do still encrease among the Inhabitants of *Rovigno* in *Istria*, I know not; yet scarce twenty Years ago Monsieur *du Loyr* observed, that a third part of that People halted: but too certain it is, that the Rickets encreaseth among us; the Small-Pox grows more pernicious than the Great: the Kings Purse knows that the King's Evil grows more common. *Quartan* Agues are become no Strangers in *Ireland*; more common and mortal in *England:* and tho the Ancients gave that Disease very good Words, yet now that Bell makes no strange sound which rings out for the Effects thereof.

Some think there were few Consumptions in the Old World, when Men lived much upon Milk; and that the ancient Inhabitants of this Island were less troubled with Coughs when they went naked, and slept in Caves and Woods, than Men now in Chambers and Feather-beds. *Plato* will tell us, that there was no such Disease as a Catarrh in *Homer*'s time, and that it was but new in *Greece* in his Age. *Polydore Virgil* delivereth that Pleurisies were rare in *England*, who lived but in the days of *Henry* the Eighth. Some will allow no Diseases to be new, others think that many old ones are ceased; and that such which are esteemed new, will have but their time: However, the Mercy of God hath scattered the great heap of Diseases, and not loaded any one Country with all: some may be new in one Country which have been old in another. New Discoveries of the Earth discover new Diseases: for besides the common swarm, there are endemial and local Infirmities proper unto certain Regions, which in the whole Earth make no small number: and if *Asia*, *Africa*, and *America* should bring in their List, *Pandoras* Box would swell, and there must be a strange Pathology.

Most Men expected to find a consumed Kell, empty and bladder-like Guts, livid and marbled Lungs, and a withered *Pericardium* in this exuccous Corps: but some seemed too much to wonder that two Lobes of his Lungs adhered unto his side; for the like I had often found in Bodies of no suspected Consumptions or difficulty of Respiration. And the same more often happeneth in Men than other Animals; and some think, in Women than in Men: but the most remarkable I have met with, was in a Man, after a Cough of almost fifty Years, in whom all the Lobes adhered unto the Pleura, and each Lobe unto another; who having also been much troubled with the Gout, brake the Rule of *Cardan*, and died of the Stone in the Bladder. *Aristotle* makes a Query, Why some Animals cough as Man, some not, as Oxen. If coughing be taken as it consisteth of a natural and voluntary motion, including Expectoration and spitting out, it may be as proper unto Man as bleeding at the Nose; otherwise we find that *Vegetius* and Rural Writers have not left so many Medicines in vain against the Coughs of Cattel; and Men who perish by Coughs dye the Death of Sheep, Cats and Lyons: and tho Birds have no Midriff, yet we meet with divers Remedies in *Arrianus* against the Coughs of Hawks. And tho it might be thought, that all Animals who have Lungs do cough; yet in cetaceous Fishes, who have large and strong Lungs, the same is not observed; nor yet in oviparous Quadrupeds: and in the greatest thereof, the Crocodile, altho we read much of their Tears, we find nothing of that motion.

From the Thoughts of Sleep, when the Soul was conceived nearest unto Divinity, the Ancients erected an Art of Divination, wherein while they too widely expatiated in loose and inconsequent Conjectures, *Hippocrates* wisely considered Dreams as they presaged Alterations in the Body, and so afforded hints toward the preservation of Health, and prevention of Diseases; and therein was so serious as to advise Alteration of Diet, Exercise, Sweating, Bathing and Vomiting; and also so religious, as to order Prayers and Supplications unto respective Deities, in good Dreams unto *Sol, Jupiter cœlestis, Jupiter opulentus, Minerva, Mercurius*, and *Apollo*; in bad unto *Tellus* and the Heroes.

And therefore I could not but take notice how his Female Friends were irrationally curious so strictly to examine his Dreams, and in this low state to hope for the Fantasms of Health. He was now past the healthful Dreams of the Sun, Moon, and Stars in their Clarity and proper Courses. 'Twas too late to dream of Flying, of Limpid Fountains, smooth Waters, white Vestments, and fruitful green Trees, which are the Visions of healthful Sleeps, and at good distance from the Grave.

And they were also too deeply dejected that he should dream of his dead Friends, inconsequently divining, that he would not be long from them; for strange it was not that he should sometimes dream of the dead whose Thoughts run always upon Death: beside, to dream of the dead, so they appear not in dark Habits, and take nothing away from us, in *Hippocrates* his Sense was of good signification: for we live by the dead, and every thing is or must be so before it becomes our Nourishment. And *Cardan*, who dream'd that he discoursed with his dead Father in the Moon, made thereof no mortal Interpretation: and even to dream that we are dead, was no condemnable Fantasm in old *Oneirocriticism*, as having a signification of Liberty, vacuity from Cares, exemption and freedom from Troubles, unknown unto the dead.

Some Dreams I confess may admit of easie and feminine Exposition: he who dream'd that he could not see his right Shoulder, might easily fear to lose the sight of his right Eye; he that before a Journey dream'd that his Feet were cut off, had a plain warning not to undertake his intended Journey. But why to dream of Lettuce should presage some ensuing Disease, why to eat Figs should signifie foolish Talk, why to eat Eggs great Trouble, and to dream of Blindness should be so highly commended, according to the *Oneirocritical* Verses of *Astrampsychus* and *Nicephorus*, I shall leave unto your Divination.

He was willing to quit the World alone and altogether, leaving no Earnest behind him for Corruption or After-grave, having small content in that common satisfaction to survive or live in another, but amply satisfied that his Disease should dye with himself, nor revive in a Posterity to puzzle Physick, and make sad *Memento's* of their Parent hereditary. Leprosie awakes not sometimes before Forty, the Gout and Stone often later; but consumptive and tabid Roots sprout more early, and at the fairest make seventeen Years of our Life doubtful before that Age. They that enter the World with original Diseases as well as Sin, have not only common Mortality but sick Traductions to destroy them, make commonly short Courses, and live not at length but in Figures; so that a sound *Cæsarean* Nativity may out-last a natural Birth, and a Knife may sometimes make way for a more lasting fruit than a Midwife; which makes so few Infants now able to endure the old Test of the River, and many to have feeble Children who could scarce have been mar-ried at *Sparta*, and those provident States who studied strong and healthful Generations; which happen but contingently in mere *pecuniary* Matches, or Marriages made by the Candle, wherein notwithstanding there is little redress to be hoped from an Astrologer or a Lawyer, and a good discerning Physician were like to prove the most successful Counsellor.

Julius Scaliger, who in a sleepless Fit of the Gout could make two hundred Verses in a Night, would have but five plain Words upon his Tomb. And this serious Person, tho no *minor* Wit, left the Poetry of his Epitaph unto others; either unwilling to commend himself, or to be judged by a Distich, and perhaps considering how unhappy great Poets have been in versifying their own Epitaphs; wherein *Petrarcha*, *Dante*, and *Ariosto*, have so unhappily failed, that if their Tombs should out-last their Works, Posterity would find so little of *Apollo* on them, as to mistake them for Ciceronian Poets.

In this deliberate and creeping progress unto the Grave, he was somewhat too young, and of too noble a mind, to fall upon that stupid Symptom observable in divers Persons near their Journeys end, and which may be reckoned among the mortal Symptoms of their last Disease; that is, to become more narrow minded, miserable and tenacious, unready to part with any thing when they are ready to part with all, and afraid to want when they have no time to spend; mean while Physicians, who know that many are mad but in a single depraved Imagination, and one prevalent Desipiency; and that beside and out of such single Deliriums a Man may meet with sober Actions and good Sense in *Bedlam;* cannot but smile to see the Heirs and concerned Relations, gratulating themselves in the sober departure of their Friends; and tho they behold such mad covetous Passages, content to think they dye in good Understanding, and in their sober Senses.

Avarice, which is not only Infidelity but Idolatry, either from covetous Progeny or questuary Education, had no Root in his Breast, who made good Works the Expression of his Faith, and was big with desires unto publick and lasting Charities; and surely where good Wishes and charitable Intentions exceed Abilities, Theorical Beneficency may be more than a Dream. They build not Castles in the Air who would build Churches on Earth; and tho they leave no such Structures here, may lay good Foundations in Heaven. In brief, his Life and Death were such, that I could not blame them who wished the like, and almost to have been himself; almost, I say; for tho we may wish the prosperous Appurtenances of others, or to be an other in his happy Accidents; yet so intrinsecal is every Man unto himself, that some doubt may be made, whether any would exchange his Being, or substantially become another Man.

He had wisely seen the World at home and abroad, and thereby observed under what variety Men are deluded in the pursuit of that which is not here to be found. And altho he had no Opinion of reputed Felicities below, and apprehended Men widely out in the estimate of such Happiness; yet his sober contempt of the World wrought no *Democritism* or *Cynicism*, no laughing or snarling at it, as well understanding there are not Felicities in this World to satisfie a serious Mind; and therefore to soften the stream of our Lives, we are fain to take in the reputed Contentations of this World, to unite with the Crowd in their Beatitudes, and to make our selves happy by

Consortion, Opinion, or Co-existimation: for strictly to separate from received and customary Felicities, and to confine unto the rigor of Realities, were to contract the Consolation of our Beings unto too uncomfortable Circumscriptions.

Not to fear Death, nor desire it, was short of his Resolution: to be dissolved, and be with Christ, was his dying ditty. He conceived his Thred long, in no long course of Years, and when he had scarce out-lived the second Life of *Lazarus;* esteeming it enough to approach the Years of his Saviour, who so ordered his own humane State, as not to be old upon Earth.

But to be content with Death may be better than to desire it: a miserable Life may make us wish for Death, but a virtuous one to rest in it; which is the Advantage of those resolved Christians, who looking on Death not only as the sting, but the period and end of Sin, the Horizon and Isthmus between this Life and a better, and the Death of this World but as a Nativity of another, do contentedly submit unto the common Necessity, and envy not *Enoch* or *Elias*.

Not to be content with Life is the unsatisfactory state of those which destroy themselves; who being afraid to live, run blindly upon their own Death, which no Man fears by Experience: and the *Stoicks* had a notable Doctrine to take away the fear thereof; that is, In such Extremities to desire that which is not to be avoided, and wish what might be feared; and so made Evils voluntary, and to suit with their own Desires, which took off the terror of them.

But the ancient Martyrs were not encouraged by such

Fallacies; who, tho they feared not Death were afraid to be their own Executioners; and therefore thought it more Wisdom to crucifie their Lusts than their Bodies, to circumcise than stab their Hearts, and to mortifie than kill themselves.

His willingness to leave this World about that Age when most Men think they may best enjoy it, tho paradoxical unto worldly Ears, was not strange unto mine, who have so often observed, that many, tho old, oft stick fast unto the World, and seem to be drawn like *Cacus's* Oxen, backward with great strugling and reluctancy unto the Grave. The long habit of Living makes meer Men more hardly to part with Life, and all to be nothing, but what is to come. To live at the rate of the old World, when some could scarce remember themselves young, may afford no better digested Death than a more moderate period. Many would have thought it an Happiness to have had their lot of Life in some notable Conjunctures of Ages past; but the uncertainty of future Times hath tempted few to make a part in Ages to come. And surely, he that hath taken the true Altitude of Things, and rightly calculated the degenerate state of this Age, is not like to envy those that shall live in the next, much less three or four hundred Years hence, when no Man can comfortably imagine what Face this World will carry: and therefore since every Age makes a step unto the end of all things, and the Scripture affords so hard a Character of the last Times; quiet Minds will be content with their Generations, and rather bless Ages past than be ambitious of those to come.

Tho Age had set no Seal upon his Face, yet a dim Eye

might clearly discover Fifty in his Actions; and therefore since Wisdom is the gray Hair, and an unspotted Life old Age; altho his Years came short, he might have been said to have held up with longer Livers, and to have been *Solomon's* Old Man. And surely if we deduct all those days of our Life which we might wish unlived, and which abate the comfort of those we now live; if we reckon up only those days which God hath accepted of our Lives, a Life of good Years will hardly be a span long: the Son in this sense may out-live the Father, and none be climaterically old. He that early arriveth unto the Parts and Prudence of Age, is happily old without the uncomfortable Attendants of it; and 'tis superfluous to live unto gray Hairs, when in a precocious Temper we anticipate the Virtues of them. In brief, he cannot be accounted young who out-liveth the old Man. He that hath early arrived unto the measure of a perfect Stature in Christ, hath already fulfilled the prime and longest Intention of his Being: and one day lived after the perfect Rule of Piety, is to be preferred before sinning Immortality.

Although he attained not unto the Years of his Predecessors, yet he wanted not those preserving Virtues which confirm the thread of weaker Constitutions. Cautelous Chastity and crafty Sobriety were far from him; those Jewels were Paragon, without Flaw, Hair, Ice, or Cloud in him: which affords me an hint to proceed in these good Wishes and few *Memento's* unto you.

Tread softly and circumspectly in this funambulous Track and narrow Path of Goodness: pursue Virtue virtuously; be sober and temperate, not to preserve your

Body in a sufficiency to wanton Ends; not to spare your Purse; not to be free from the Infamy of common Transgressors that way, and thereby to ballance or palliate obscure and closer Vices; nor simply to enjoy Health: by all which you may leaven good Actions, and render Virtues disputable: but in one Word, that you may truly serve God; which every Sickness will tell you, you cannot well do without Health. The sick mans Sacrifice is but a lame Oblation. Pious Treasures laid up in healthful days, excuse the defect of sick Non-performances; without which we must needs look back with Anxiety upon the lost opportunities of Health; and may have cause rather to envy than pity the Ends of penitent Malefactors, who go with clear parts unto the last Act of their Lives; and in the integrity of their Faculties return their Spirit unto God that gave it.

Consider whereabout thou art in *Cebes* his Table, or that old philosophical Pinax of the Life of Man; whether thou art still in the Road of Uncertainties; whether thou hast yet entred the narrow Gate, got up the Hill and asperous way which leadeth unto the House of Sanity, or taken that purifying Potion from the hand of sincere Erudition, which may send thee clear and pure a way unto a virtuous and happy Life.

In this virtuous Voyage let not disappointment cause Despondency, nor difficulty Despair: think not that you are sailing from *Lima* to *Manillia*, wherein thou may'st tye up the Rudder, and sleep before the Wind; but expect rough Seas, Flaws, and contrary Blasts; and 'tis well if by many cross Tacks and Verings thou arrivest at thy Port. Sit not down in the popular Seats and common Level of

Virtues, but endeavour to make them Heroical. Offer not only Peace-Offerings but Holocausts unto God. To serve him singly, to serve our selves; were too partial a piece of Piety, nor likely to place us in the highest Mansions of Glory.

He that is chaste and continent, not to impair his Strength, or terrified by Contagion, will hardly be heroically virtuous. Adjourn not that Virtue unto those Years when *Cato* could lend out his Wife, and impotent Satyrs write Satyrs against Lust: but be chaste in thy flaming days, when *Alexander* dared not trust his Eyes upon the fair Daughters of *Darius*, and when so many Men think there is no other way but *Origen's*.

Be charitable before Wealth makes thee covetous, and lose not the Glory of the Mite. If Riches increase, let thy Mind hold pace with them; and think it not enough to be liberal, but munificent. Tho a Cup of cold Water from some hand may not be without its Reward; yet stick not thou for Wine and Oyl for the Wounds of the distressed: and treat the Poor as our Saviour did the Multitude, to the Relicks of some Baskets.

Trust not to the Omnipotency of Gold, or say unto it, Thou art my Confidence: Kiss not thy Hand when thou beholdest that terrestrial Sun, nor bore thy Ear unto its Servitude. A Slave unto Mammon makes no Servant unto God: Covetousness cracks the Sinews of Faith, numbs the Apprehension of any thing above Sense, and only affected with the certainty of things present, makes a peradventure of Things to come; lives but unto one World, nor hopes but fears another; makes our own Death sweet unto others, bitter unto our selves; gives a dry Funeral, Scenical Mourning, and no wet Eyes at the Grave.

If Avarice be thy Vice, yet make it not thy Punishment: miserable Men commiserate not themselves, bowelless unto themselves, and merciless unto their own Bowels. Let the fruition of Things bless the possession of them, and take no satisfaction in dying but living rich: for since thy good Works, not thy Goods, will follow thee; since Riches are an Appurtenance of Life, and no dead Man is rich, to famish in Plenty, and live poorly to dye rich, were a multiplying improvement in Madness, and Use upon Use in Folly.

Persons lightly dip'd, not grain'd in generous Honesty, are but pale in Goodness, and faint hued in Sincerity: but be thou what thou virtuously art, and let not the Ocean wash away thy Tincture: stand magnetically upon that Axis where prudent Simplicity hath fix'd thee, and let no Temptation invert the Poles of thy Honesty: and that Vice may be uneasie, and even monstrous unto thee, let iterated good Acts, and long confirmed Habits, make Vertue natural, or a second Nature in thee. And since few or none prove eminently vertuous but from some advantageous Foundations in their Temper and natural Inclinations; study thy self betimes, and early find, what Nature bids thee to be, or tells thee what thou may'st be. They who thus timely descend into themselves, cultivating the good Seeds which Nature hath set in them, and improving their prevalent Inclinations to Perfection, become not Shrubs, but Cedars in their Generation; and to be in the form of the best of the Bad, or the worst of the Good, will be no satisfaction unto them.

Let not the Law of thy Country be the *non ultra* of thy Honesty, nor think that always good enough which the Law will make good. Narrow not the Law of Charity, Equity, Mercy; joyn Gospel Righteousness with Legal Right; be not a meer *Gamaliel* in the Faith; but let the Sermon in the Mount be thy *Targum* unto the Law of *Sinai*.

Make not the Consequences of Vertue the Ends thereof: be not beneficent for a Name or Cymbal of Applause, nor exact and punctual in Commerce, for the Advantages of Trust and Credit, which attend the Reputation of just and true Dealing; for such Rewards, tho unsought for, plain Virtue will bring with her, whom all Men honour, tho they pursue not. To have other bye ends in good Actions, sowers laudable Performances, which must have deeper Roots, Motions, and Instigations, to give them the Stamp of Vertues.

Tho humane Infirmity may betray thy heedless days into the popular ways of Extravagancy, yet let not thine own depravity, or the torrent of vicious Times, carry thee into desperate Enormities in Opinions, Manners, or Actions: if thou hast dip'd thy foot in the River, yet venture not over *Rubicon*; run not into Extremities from whence there is no Regression, nor be ever so closely shut up within the holds of Vice and Iniquity, as not to find some Escape by a Postern of Resipiscency.

Owe not thy Humility unto Humiliation by Adversity, but look humbly down in that State when others look upward upon thee: be patient in the Age of Pride and days of Will and Impatiency, when Men live but by Intervals of Reason, under the Sovereignty of Humor and Passion, when 'tis in the Power of every one to transform thee out of thy self, and put thee into the short Madness. If you cannot imitate *Job*, yet come not short of *Socrates*, and those patient Pagans, who tired the Tongues of their Enemies, while they perceiv'd they spet their Malice at brazen Walls and Statues.

Let Age, not Envy, draw Wrinkles on thy Cheeks: be content to be envied, but envy not. Emulation may be plausible, and Indignation allowable; but admit no Treaty with that Passion which no Circumstance can make good. A Displacency at the good of others, because they enjoy it, altho we do not want it, is an absurd Depravity, sticking fast unto humane Nature from its primitive Corruption; which he that can well subdue, were a Christian of the first Magnitude, and for ought I know, may have one foot already in Heaven.

While thou so hotly disclaimst the Devil, be not guilty of Diabolism; fall not into one Name with that unclean Spirit, nor act his Nature whom thou so much abhorrest; that is, to accuse, calumniate, backbite, whisper, detract, or sinistrously interpret others; degenerous Depravities and narrow-minded Vices, not only below *S. Paul*'s noble Christian, but *Aristotle*'s true Gentleman. Trust not with some, that the Epistle of *S. James* is Apocryphal, and so read with less fear that stabbing truth, that in company with this Vice thy Religion is in vain. *Moses* broke the Tables without breaking of the Law; but where Charity is broke the Law it self is shattered, which cannot be whole without Love, that is the fulfilling of it. Look humbly upon thy Virtues, and tho thou art rich in some, yet think thy self poor and naked without that crowning

Grace, which thinketh no Evil, which envieth not, which beareth, believeth, hopeth, endureth all things. With these sure Graces, while busie Tongues are crying out for a drop of cold Water, Mutes may be in Happiness, and sing the *Trisagium* in Heaven.

Let not the Sun in *Capricorn* go down upon thy Wrath, but write thy Wrongs in Water; draw the Curtain of Night upon Injuries; shut them up in the Tower of Oblivion, and let them be as tho they had not been. Forgive thine Enemies totally, and without any Reserve of hope, that however, God will revenge thee.

Be substantially great in thy self, and more than thou appearest unto others; and let the World be deceived in thee, as they are in the Lights of Heaven. Hang early Plummets upon the Heels of Pride, and let Ambition have but an Epicycle or narrow Circuit in thee. Measure not thy self by thy Morning shadow, but by the Extent of thy Grave; and reckon thy self above the Earth by the Line thou must be contented with under it. Spread not into boundless Expansions either of Designs or Desires. Think not that Mankind liveth but for a few, and that the rest are born but to serve the Ambition of those, who make but Flies of Men, and Wildernesses of whole Nations. Swell not into Actions which embroil and confound the Earth; but be one of those violent ones which force the Kingdom of Heaven. If thou must needs reign, be *Zeno*'s King, and enjoy that Empire which every Man gives himself. Certainly the iterated Injunctions of Christ unto Humility, Meekness, Patience, and that despised Train of Virtues, cannot but make pathetical Impressions upon those who have well considered the Affairs of all Ages, wherein Pride, Ambition, and Vain-glory, have led up the worst of Actions, and whereunto Confusion, Tragedies, and Acts denying all Religion, do owe their Originals.

Rest not in an Ovation, but a Triumph over thy Passions; chain up the unruly Legion of thy Breast; behold thy Trophies within thee, not without thee: Lead thine own Captivity captive, and be *Cæsar* unto thy self.

Give no quarter unto those Vices which are of thine inward Family: and having a Root in thy Temper, plead a Right and Propriety in thee. Examine well thy complexional Inclinations. Raise early Batteries against those strong-holds built upon the Rock of Nature, and make this a great part of the Militia of thy Life. The politick Nature of Vice must be opposed by Policy, and therefore wiser Honesties Project and plot against Sin; wherein notwithstanding we are not to rest in Generals, or the trite Stratagems of Art: that may succeed with one Temper which may prove successless with another. There is no Community or Commonwealth of Virtue; every Man must study his own OEconomy, and erect these Rules unto the Figure of himself.

Lastly, If length of Days be thy Portion, make it not thy Expectation: reckon not upon long Life, but live always beyond thy Account. He that so often surviveth his Expectation, lives many Lives, and will hardly complain of the shortness of his Days. Time past is gone like a shadow; make Times to come, present; conceive that near which may be far off; approximate thy last Times by present Apprehensions of them: live like a Neighbour unto Death, and think there is but little to come. And since there is something in us that must still live on, joyn both Lives together; unite them in thy Thoughts and Actions, and live in one but for the other. He who thus ordereth the Purposes of this Life, will never be far from the next; and is in some manner already in it, by an happy Conformity, and close Apprehension of it.

from Religio Medici

That Miracles are ceased, I can neither prove, nor absolutely deny, much lesse define the time and period of their cessation; that they survived Christ, is manifest upon record of Scripture; that they out-lived the Apostles also, and were revived at the conversion of Nations, many yeares after, we cannot deny, if wee shall not question those Writers whose testimonies wee doe not controvert, in points that make for our owne opinions; therefore that may have some truth in it that is reported of the Jesuites and their Miracles in the Indies, I could wish it were true, or had any other testimony then their owne Pennes: they may easily beleeve those Miracles abroad, who daily conceive a greater at home; the transmutation of those visible elements into the body and blood of our Saviour: for the conversion of water into wine, which he wrought in *Cana*, or what the Devill would have had him do in the wildernesse, of stones into Bread, compared to this, will scarce deserve the name of a Miracle: Though indeed, to speake strictly, there is not one Miracle greater than another, they being the extraordinary effects of the hand of God, to which all things are of an equall facility; and to create the world as easie as one single creature. For this is also a miracle, not onely to produce effects against, or above Nature, but before Nature; and to create Nature as great a miracle, as to contradict or transcend her. Wee doe too narrowly define the power of God, restraining it to our capacities. I hold that God can doe all things, how he should work contradictions I do not understand, yet dare not therefore deny. I cannot see why the Angel of God should question *Esdras* to recall the time past, if it were beyond his owne power; or that God should pose mortalitie in that, which hee could not performe himselfe. I will not say God cannot, but hee will not performe many things, which wee plainely affirme he cannot: this I am sure is the mannerliest proposition, wherein notwithstanding I hold no Paradox. For strictly his power is [but] the same with his will, and they both with all the rest doe make but one God.

[. . .]

I am naturally bashfull, nor hath conversation, age, or travell, beene able to effront, or enharden me; yet I have one part of modesty, which I have seldome discovered in another, that is (to speake truly) I am not so much afraid of death, as ashamed thereof; tis the very disgrace and ignominy of our natures, that in a moment can so disfigure us that our nearest friends, wives and Children stand afraid and start at us. The Birds and Beasts of the field that before in a naturall feare obeyed us, forgetting all allegiance begin to prey upon us. This very conceite hath in a tempest disposed and left me willing to be swallowed in the abysse of waters; wherein I had perished unseene, unpityed, without wondring eyes, teares of pity, Lectures of mortality, and none had said, *quantum mutatus ab illo!* Not that I am ashamed of the Anatomy of my parts, or can accuse nature for playing the bungler in any part of me, or my owne vitious life for contracting any shamefull disease upon me, whereby I might not call my selfe as wholesome a morsell for the wormes as any.

[...]

Now for the wals of flesh, wherein the soule doth seeme to be immured before the Resurrection, it is nothing but an elementall composition, and a fabricke that must fall to ashes; *All flesh is grasse*, is not onely metaphorically, but literally true, for all those creatures which we behold, are but the hearbs of the field, digested into flesh in them, or more remotely carnified in our selves. Nay further, we are what we all abhorre, *Antropophagi* and Cannibals, devourers not onely of men, but of our selves; and that not in an allegory, but a positive truth; for all this masse of flesh which wee behold, came in at our mouths: this frame wee looke upon, hath beene upon our trenchers; In briefe, we have devoured our selves and yet do live and remaine our selves. I cannot beleeve the wisedome of *Pythagoras* did ever positively, and in a literall sense, affirme his *Metempsychosis*, or impossible transmigration of the soules of men into beasts: of all Metamorphoses and transformations, I beleeve onely one, that is of *Lots* wife, for that of *Nabuchodonosor* proceeded not so farre; In all others I conceive there is no further verity then is contained in their implicite sense and morality: I beleeve that the whole frame of a beast doth perish, and is left in the same state after death, as before it was materialled unto life; that the soules of men know neither contrary nor corruption, that they subsist beyond the body, and outlive death by the priviledge of their proper natures, and without a miracle; that the soules of the faithfull as they leave earth, take possession of Heaven: that those apparitions, and ghosts of departed persons, are not the wandring soules of men, but the unquiet walkes of Devils, prompting and suggesting us unto mischiefe, bloud, and villany; instilling, & stealing into our hearts, that the blessed spirits are not at rest in their graves, but wander solicitous of the affaires of the world. That those phantasmes appeare often, and doe frequent Cemiteries, charnall houses, and Churches, it is because those are the dormitories of the dead, where the Devill like an insolent Champion beholds with pride the spoyles and Trophies of his victory in *Adam*.

This is that dismall conquest we all deplore, that makes us so often cry (O) *Adam, quid fecisti?* [Adam, what hast thou done?] I thanke God I have not those strait ligaments, or narrow obligations to the world, as to dote on life, or be convulst and tremble at the name of death: Not that I am insensible of the dread and horrour thereof, or by raking into the bowells of the deceased, [or the] continual sight of Anatomies, Skeletons, or Cadaverous reliques, like Vespilloes or Grave-makers, I am become stupid, or have forgot the apprehension of mortality; but that marshalling all the horrours, and contemplating the extremities thereof, I finde not any thing therein able to daunt the courage of a man, much lesse a well resolved Christian. And therefore am not angry at the errour of our first parents, or unwilling to beare a part in this common fate, and like the best of them to dye; that is, to cease to breathe, to take a farewell of the elements, to be a kinde of nothing for a moment, to be within one instant a spirit. When I take a full view and circle of my selfe, without this reasonable moderator, and equal piece of justice, Death, I doe conceive my selfe the miserablest person extant; were there not another life that I hope for, all the vanities of this world should not intreat a moments breath from me; could the Devill worke my beliefe to imagine I could never dye, I would not out-live that very thought; I have so abject a conceit of this common way of existence, this retaining to the Sunne and Elements, I cannot thinke this is to be a man, or to live according to the dignitie of humanity; in expectation of a better I can with patience embrace this life; yet in my best meditations doe often desire death; It is a symptom of melancholy to be afraid of death, yet sometimes to desire it; this latter I have often discovered in my selfe, and thinke no man ever desired life as I have sometimes death. I honour any man that contemnes it, nor can I highly love any that is afraid of it; this makes me naturally love a Souldier, and honour those tattered and contemptible Regiments that will die at the command of a Sergeant. For a Pagan there may bee some motives to bee in love with life; but for a Christian that is amazed at death, I see not how hee can escape this Dilemma: that he is too sensible of this life, or hopelesse of the life to come.

Sir Thomas Browne

[. . .]

It is not, I confesse, an unlawfull Prayer to desire to
surpasse the dayes of our Saviour, or wish to out-live
that age wherein he thought fittest to dye; yet if (as
Divinity affirmes) there shall be no gray hayres in
Heaven, but all shall rise in the perfect state of men, we
doe but out-live those perfections in this world, to be
recalled unto them by a greater miracle in the next, and
run on here but to be retrograde hereafter. Were there
any hopes to out-live vice, or a point to be superannuated from sin, it were worthy [of] our knees to
implore the dayes of *Methuselah*. But age doth not rectifie,
but incurvate our natures, turning bad dispositions into
worser habits, and (like diseases) brings on incurable
vices; for every day as we grow weaker in age, we grow
stronger in sinne, and the number of our dayes doth but
make our sinnes innumerable. The same vice committed
at sixteene, is not the same, though it agree in all other
circumstances, at forty; but swels and doubles from the
circumstance of our ages, wherein besides the constant
and inexcusable habit of transgressing, the maturity of
our Judgement cuts off pretence unto excuse or pardon:
every sin, the oftner it is committed, the more it
acquireth in the quality of evill; as it succeeds in time, so
it proceeds in degrees of badnesse; for as they proceed
they ever multiply, and like figures in Arithmeticke, the
last stands for more than all that went before it:[1] And
though I thinke no man can live well once but hee that
could live twice, yet, for my owne part, I would not live
over my houres past, or beginne againe the thred of my

dayes: not upon *Cicero*'s ground, because I have lived them well, but for feare I should live them worse; I find my growing Judgement dayly instructs me how to be better, but my untamed affections and confirmed vitiosity make mee dayly doe worse; I finde in my confirmed age the same sinnes I discovered in my youth; I committed many then because I was a child, and because I commit them still I am yet an Infant. Therefore I perceive a man may bee twice a child before the dayes of dotage, and stand in need of *Aesons* bath before threescore.

[...]

Men commonly set forth the tortures of Hell by fire, and the extremitie of corporall afflictions, and describe Hell in the same manner as *Mahomet* doth Heaven. This indeed makes a noyse, and drums in popular eares: but if this be the terrible piece thereof, it is not worthy to stand in diameter with Heaven, whose happinesse consists in that part which is best able to comprehend it, that immortall essence, that translated divinity and colony of God, the soule. Surely though wee place Hell under earth, the Devils walke and purlue is about it; men speake too popularly who place it in those flaming mountaines, which to grosser apprehensions represent Hell. The heart of man is the place the devill dwels in; I feele somtimes a hell within my selfe, *Lucifer* keeps his court in my brest, Legion is revived in me. There are as many hels as *Anaxagoras* conceited worlds; there was more than one hell in *Magdalen*, when there were seven devils; for every devill is an hell unto himself: hee holds enough of torture in his owne *ubi*, and needs not the misery of circumference to afflict him, and thus a distracted conscience here is a shadow or introduction unto hell hereafter; Who can but pity the mercifull intention of those hands that doe destroy themselves? the devill, were it in his power, would doe the like; which being impossible, his miseries are endlesse, and he suffers most in that attribute, wherein he is impassible, his immortality.

[. . .]

The number of those who pretend unto salvation, and those infinite swarmes who thinke to passe through the eye of this Needle, have much amazed me. That name and compellation of *little Flocke*, doth not comfort but deject my devotion, especially when I reflect upon mine owne unworthinesse, wherein, according to my humble apprehension, I am below them all. I beleeve there shall never be an Anarchy in Heaven, but as there are Hierarchies amongst the Angels, so shall there be degrees of priority amongst the Saints. Yet is it (I protest) beyond my ambition to aspire unto the first rankes; my desires onely are, and I shall be happy therein, to be but the last man, and bring up the Rere in Heaven.

Againe, I am confident and fully perswaded, yet dare not take my oath of my salvation; I am as it were sure, and do beleeve, without all doubt, that there is such a city as *Constantinople*; yet for me to take my oath thereon, were a kinde of perjury, because I hold no infallible warrant from my owne sense, to confirme me in the certainty thereof. And truely, though many pretend an absolute certainty of their salvation, yet when an humble soule shall contemplate her owne unworthinesse, she shall meete with many doubts and suddainely finde how much wee stand in need of the precept of Saint *Paul, Worke out your salvation with feare and trembling*. That which is the cause of my election, I hold to be the cause of my salvation, which was the mercy, and beneplacit of God, before I was, or the foundation of the world. *Before Abraham was, I am*, is the saying of Christ; yet is it true in some sense if I say it of my selfe, for I was not onely before my selfe, but *Adam*, that is, in the Idea of God, and the decree of that Synod held from all Eternity. And in this sense, I say, the world was before the Creation, and at an end before it had a beginning; and thus was I dead before I was alive; though my grave be *England*, my dying place was Paradise, and *Eve* miscarried of mee before she conceiv'd of *Cain*.

[. . .]

It is the common wonder of all men, how among so many millions of faces, there should be none alike; Now contrary, I wonder as much how there should be any; he that shall consider how many thousand severall words have beene carelesly and without study composed out of 24 Letters; withall how many hundred lines there are to be drawn in the fabrick of one man; shall easily finde that this variety is necessary: And it will bee very hard that they should so concur as to make one portract like another. Let a Painter carelesly limn out a Million of faces, and you shall finde them all different; yea let him have his copy before him, yet after all his art there will remaine a sensible distinction; for the pattern or example of every thing is the perfectest in that kind, whereof wee still come short, though wee transcend or goe beyond it, because herein it is wide and agrees not in all points unto its Copy. I rather wonder how almost all plants being of one colour, yet should bee all different herein, and their severall kinds distinguished in one accident of verte. Nor doth the similitude of creatures disparage the variety of nature, nor any way confound the workes of God. For even in things alike, there is diversitie, and those that doe seeme to accord, doe manifestly disagree. And thus is Man like God, for in the same things that wee resemble him, wee are utterly different from him. There is never any thing so like another, as in all points to concurre; there will ever some reserved difference slip in, to prevent the Identity, without which two severall things would not be alike, but the same, which is impossible.

[. . .]

I thanke God, amongst those millions of vices I doe inherit and hold from *Adam*, I have escaped one, and that a mortall enemy to charity, the first and father sin, not only of man, but of the devil: Pride. A vice whose name is comprehended in a Monosyllable, but in its nature circumscribed not with a world; I have escaped it in a condition that can hardly avoid it: those petty acquisitions and reputed perfections that advance and elevate the conceits of other men, adde no feathers unto mine; I have seene a Grammarian towr, and plume himselfe over a single line in *Horace*, and shew more pride in the construction of one Ode, than the Author in the composure of the whole book. For my owne part, besides the *Jargon* and *Patois* of severall Provinces, I understand no less then six Languages; yet I protest I have no higher conceit of my selfe than had our Fathers before the confusion of *Babel*, when there was but one Language in the world, and none to boast himselfe either Linguist or Criticke. I have not onely seene severall Countries, beheld the nature of their climes, the Chorography of their Provinces, Topography of their Cities, but understand their severall Lawes, Customes and Policies; yet cannot all this perswade the dulnesse of my spirit unto such an opinion of my self, as I behold in nimbler & conceited heads, that never looked a degree beyond their nests. I know the names, and somewhat more, of all the constellations in my Horizon, yet I have seene a prating Mariner that could onely name the Poynters and the North Starre, out-talke mee, and conceit himselfe a whole Spheare above mee. I know most of the Plants of my Country, and of those about mee; yet me thinkes I do not know so many as when I did but know an hundred, and had scarcely ever Simpled further than Cheap-side: for indeed heads of capacity, and such as are not full with a handfull, or easie measure of knowledg, thinke they know nothing, till they know all; which being impossible, they fall upon the opinion of *Socrates*, and onely know they know not any thing.

I cannot thinke that *Homer* pin'd away upon the riddle of the Fishermen, or that *Aristotle*, who understood the uncertainty of knowledge, and so often confessed the reason of man too weake for the workes of nature, did ever drowne himselfe upon the flux and reflux of *Euripus:* wee doe but learne to day, what our better advanced judgements will unteach us to morrow: and *Aristotle* doth but instruct us as *Plato* did him; that is, to confute himselfe. I have runne through all sorts, yet finde no rest in any; though our first studies & *junior* endeavors may stile us Peripateticks, Stoicks, or Academicks, yet I perceive the wisest heads prove at last, almost all Scepticks, and stand like *Janus* in the field of knowledge. I have therefore one common and authentick Philosophy I learned in the Schooles, whereby I discourse and satisfie the reason of other men; another more reserved and drawne from experience whereby I content mine owne. *Solomon* that complained of ignorance in the height of knowledge, hath not onely humbled my conceits, but discouraged my endeavours. There is yet another conceit that hath sometimes made me shut my bookes; which tels mee it is a vanity to waste our dayes in the blind pursuit of knowledge; it is but attending a little longer, and wee shall enjoy that by instinct and infusion which we endeavour at here by labour and inquisition: it is better to sit downe in a modest ignorance, & rest contented with the naturall blessing of our owne reasons, then buy the uncertaine knowledge of this life, with sweat and vexation, which death gives every foole gratis, and is an accessary of our glorification.

[. . .]

Now for my life, it is a miracle of thirty yeares, which to relate, were not a History, but a peece of Poetry, and would sound to common eares like a fable; for the world, I count it not an Inne, but an Hospitall, and a place, not to live, but to die in. The world that I regard is my selfe, it is the Microcosme of mine owne frame, that I cast mine eye on; for the other, I use it but like my Globe, and turne it round sometimes for my recreation. Men that look upon my outside, perusing onely my condition, and fortunes, do erre in my altitude; for I am above *Atlas* his shoulders, and though I seeme on earth to stand, on tiptoe in Heaven. The earth is a point not onely in respect of the heavens above us, but of that heavenly and celestiall part within us: that masse of flesh that circumscribes me, limits not my mind: that surface that tells the heavens it hath an end, cannot perswade me I have any; I take my circle to be above three hundred and sixty; though the number of the Arke do measure my body, it comprehendeth not my minde: whilst I study to finde how I am a Microcosme or little world, I finde my selfe something more than the great. There is surely a peece of Divinity in us, something that was before the Elements, and owes no homage unto the Sun. Nature tels me I am the Image of God as well as Scripture; he that understands not thus much, hath not his introduction or first lesson, and is yet to begin the Alphabet of man. Let me not injure the felicity of others, if I say I am as happy as any. I have that in me that can convert poverty into riches, transforme adversity into prosperity. I am more invulnerable than Achilles. Fortune hath not one place to hit me. *Ruat coelum, Fiat voluntas tua* [Though the heavens fall, thy will be done] salveth all; so that whatsoever happens, it is but what our daily prayers desire. In briefe, I am content, and what should providence adde more? Surely this is it wee call Happinesse, and this doe I enjoy, with this I am happy in a dreame, and as content to enjoy a happinesse in a fancie as others in a more apparent truth and reality. There is surely a neerer apprehension of any thing that delights us in our dreames, than in our waked senses: with this I can be a king without a crown, rich without a stiver; in Heaven though on earth; enjoy my friend and embrace him at a distance, when I cannot behold him; without this I were unhappy, for my awaked judgement discontents me, ever whispering unto me, that I am from my friend; but my friendly dreames in the night requite me, and make me thinke I am within his armes. I thanke God for my happy dreames, as I doe for my good rest, for there is a satisfaction in them unto reasonable desires, and such as can be content with a fit of happinesse; and surely it is not a melancholy conceite to thinke we are all asleepe in this world, and that the conceits of this life are as meare dreames to those of the next, as the Phantasmes of the night, to the conceits of the day. There is an equall delusion in both, and the one doth but seeme to bee the embleme and picture of the other; we are somewhat more than our selves in our sleepes, and the slumber of the body seemes to bee but the waking of the soule. It is the ligation of sense, but the liberty of reason, and our waking conceptions doe not match the fancies of our

sleepes. At my Nativity, my ascendant was the watery
signe of *Scorpius*; I was borne in the Planetary houre of
Saturne, and I think I have a peece of that Leaden Planet
in me. I am no way facetious, nor disposed for the mirth
and galliardize of company; yet in one dreame I can
compose a whole Comedy, behold the action, apprehend
the jests, and laugh my selfe awake at the conceits
thereof; were my memory as faithfull as my reason is
then fruitfull, I would never study but in my dreames,
and this time also would I chuse for my devotions; but
our grosser memories have then so little hold of our
abstracted understandings, that they forget the story,
and can only relate to our awaked soules, a confused &
broken tale of what hath passed. *Aristotle*, who hath
written a singular tract of sleepe, hath not me thinkes
throughly defined it, nor yet *Galen*, though hee seeme
to have corrected it; for those *Noctambuloes* or night-
walkers, though in their sleepe, doe yet enjoy the action
of their senses; wee must therefore say that there is
something in us that is not in the jurisdiction of *Morpheus*;
and that those abstracted and ecstaticke soules doe walke
about in their owne corps, as spirits in the bodies they
assume, wherein they seeme to heare, see and feele,
though indeed the organs are destitute of sense, and
their natures of those faculties that should informe them.
Thus it is observed that men sometimes upon the houre
of their departure, doe speake and reason above themselves. For then the soule beginning to bee freed from
the ligaments of the body, begins to reason like her selfe,
and to discourse in a straine above mortality.

from Enquiries into Very Many Received Tenets and Commonly Presumed Truths

Of the Elephant

The first shall be of the Elephant; whereof there generally passeth an opinion it hath no joints; and this absurdity is seconded with another, that being unable to lie down, it sleepeth against a tree; which the Hunters observing doe saw almost asunder; whereon the beast relying, by the fall of the tree falls also down it self, and is able to rise no more. Which conceit is not the daughter of later times, but an old and gray-headed error, even in the daies of Aristotle, as he delivereth in his book, *de incessu animalium*; and stand successively related by severall other Authors; by Diodorus Siculus, Strabo, Ambrose, Cassiodore, Solinus and many more. Now herein me thinks men much forget themselves, not well considering the absurdity of such assertions.

For first, they affirm it hath no joints, and yet concede it walks and moves about; whereby they conceive there may be a progression or advancement made in motion without inflexion of parts. Now all progression or animall locomotion being (as Aristotle teacheth) performed *tractu & pulsu*; that is, by drawing on, or impelling forward some part which was before in station, or at quiet; where there are no joints or flexures, neither can there be these actions; and this is true, not only in Quadrupedes, Volatils and Fishes, which have distinct and prominent organs of motion, legs, wings and fins; but in such also as perform their progression by the trunck, as Serpents, Wormes and Leeches; whereof though some want bones, and all extended articulations, yet have they arthriticall analogies; and by the motion of fibrous and musculous parts, are able to make progression. Which to conceive in bodies inflexible, and without all protrusion of parts, were to expect a race from Hercules his pillars; or hope to behold the effects of Orpheus his harp; when Trees found joints, and danced after his musick.

Again, While men conceive they never lie down, and enjoy not the position of rest, ordained unto all pedestrious animals, hereby they imagin (what reason cannot conceive) that an animall of the vastest dimension and longest duration, should live in a continuall motion, without that alternity and vicissitude of rest whereby all others continue; and yet must thus much come to passe, if we opinion they lie not down and enjoy no decumbence at all. For station is properly no rest, but one kinde of motion, relating unto that which Physitians (from Galen) doe name extensive or tonicall; that is, an extension of the muscles and organs of motion maintaining the body at length or in its proper figure; wherein although it seem to be unmoved, it is neverthelesse not without all motion; for in this position the muscles are sensibly extended, and labour to support the body; which permitted unto its proper gravity, would suddenly subside and fall unto the earth, as it happeneth in sleep, diseases and death. From which occult action and invisible motion of the muscles in station (as Galen declareth) proceed more offensive lassitudes then from ambulation. And therefore the Tyranny of some have tormented men, with long and enforced station; and though Ixion and Sisiphus which alwaies moved, doe seem to have the hardest measure: yet was not Titius favoured, that lay extended upon Caucasus; and Tantalus suffered somewhat more then thirst, that stood perpetually in hell. Thus Mercurialis in his Gymnasticks justly makes standing one kinde of exercise; and Galen when we lye down, commends unto us middle figures; that is, not to lye directly, or at length, but somewhat inflected, that the muscles may be at rest; for such as he termeth Hypobolemaioi or figures of excesse, either shrinking up or stretching out, are wearisome positions, and such as perturb the quiet of those parts. Now various parts doe variously discover these indolent and quiet positions; some in right lines, as the wrists; some at right angles, as the cubit; others at oblique angles, as the fingers and the knees: all resting satisfied in postures of moderation, and none enduring the extremity of flexure or extension.

Moreover men herein doe strangely forget the obvious relations of history, affirming they have no joints, whereas they daily reade of severall actions which are not performable without them. They forget what is delivered by Xiphilinus, and also by Suetonius in the lives of Nero and Galba, that Elephants have been instructed to walk on ropes, in publike shews before the people; which is not easily performed by man, and

requireth not only a broad foot, but a pliable flexure
of joints, and commandible disposure of all parts of
progression. They passe by that memorable place in
Curtius, concerning the Elephant of King Porus, *Indus
qui Elephantem regebat, descendere eum ratus, more solito
procumbere jussit in genua, cæteri quoque (ita enim instituti
erant) demisere corpora in terram.** They remember not
the expression of *Osorius de rebus gestis Emanuelis*, when
he speaks of the Elephant presented to Leo the tenth,
*Pontificem ter genibus flexis, & demisso corporis habitu vener-
abundus salutavit.*† But above all, they call not to minde
that memorable shew of Germanicus, wherein twelve
Elephants danced unto the sound of musick, and after
laid them down in the Tricliniums, or places of festivall
Recumbency.

They forget the Etymologie of the Knee, approved by
some Grammarians. They disturb the position of the
young ones in the wombe: which upon extension of
leggs is not easily conceiveable; and contrary unto the
generall contrivance of nature. Nor doe they consider
the impossible exclusion thereof, upon extension and
rigour of the leggs.

Lastly, They forget or consult not experience; whereof
not many years past, we have had the advantage in
England, by an Elephant shewn in many parts thereof;

* 'The Indian who controlled the elephant, intending to dismount,
in the usual way ordered it to go down on its knees, and all the others
let their bodies down on the ground, because they had been trained
to do so.'
† 'It greeted the bishop with venetation, kneeling three times and
keeping itself in a lowly position.'

not only in the posture of standing, but kneeling and lying down. Whereby although the opinion at present be well suppressed, yet from some strings of tradition, and fruitfull recurrence of error, it is not improbable, it may revive in the next generation again; this being not the first that hath been seen in England; for (besides some other since) as Polydore Virgil relateth, Lewis the French King sent one to Henry the third; and Emanuel of Portugall another to Leo the tenth into Italy; where notwithstanding the error is still alive and epidemicall, as with us.

The hint and ground of this opinion might be the grosse and somewhat Cylindricall composure of the legs, the equality and lesse perceptible disposure of the joints, especially in the four legs of this Animall; they appearing when he standeth, like pillars of flesh, without any evidence of articulation. The different flexure and order of the joints might also countenance the same; being not disposed in the Elephant, as they are in other quandrupedes, but carry a nearer conformity into those of man; that is; the bought of the fore-legs not directly backward, but laterally and somewhat inward; but the hough or suffraginous flexure behinde rather outward. Contrary unto many other quadrupedes, and such as can scratch the ear with the hinder foot, as Horses, Camels, Deer, Sheep and Dogges; for their fore legs bend like our legs, and their hinder legs like our arms, when we move them to our shoulders. But quadrupedes oviparous, as Frogs, Lizards, Crocadiles, have their joints and motive flexures more analogously framed unto ours; and some among viviparous; that is, such thereof as can bring their fore-feet and meat therein into their mouthes, as most can doe that have the clavicles or coller-bones; whereby their breasts are broader, and their shoulders more asunder, as the Ape, the Monkey, the Squirrell and some others. If therefore any shall affirm the joints of Elephants are differently framed from most of other quadrupedes, and more obscurely and grossely almost then any; he doth herein no injury unto truth. But if *à dicto secundum quid ad dictum simpliciter*, he affirmeth also they have no articulations at all; he incurs the controllment of reason, and cannot avoid the contradiction also of sense.

As for the manner of their venation, if we consult historicall experience, we shall finde it to be otherwise then as is commonly presumed, by sawing away of trees. The accounts whereof are to be seen at large in *Johannes Hugo, Edwardus Lopez, Garcias ab Horto, Cadamustus* and many more.

Other concernments there are of the Elephant, which might admit of discourse; and if we should question the teeth of Elephants, that is, whether they be properly so termed, or might not rather be called horns; it were no new enquiry of mine, but a paradox as old as Oppianus. Whether as Pliny and divers since affirm, that Elephants are terrefied, and make away upon the grunting of Swine, *Garcias ab Horto* may decide, who affirmeth upon experience they enter their stalls, and live promiscuously in the woods of Malavar. That the situation of the genitalls is averse, and their copulation like that of Camels, as Pliny hath also delivered, is not to be received; for we have beheld that part in a different position; and their coition is made by supersaliency like that of Horses, as we are informed by some who have beheld them in that act. That some Elephants have not only written whole sentences, as Ælian ocularly testifieth, but have also spoken, as Oppianus delivereth, and Christophorus a Costa particularly relateth; although it sound like that of Achilles Horse in Homer, we doe not conceive impossible: nor beside the affinity of reason in this Animall any such intollerable incapacity in the organs of divers quadrupedes, whereby they might not be taught to speak, or become imitators of speech like birds. Strange it is how the curiosity of men that have been active in the instruction of beasts, have never fallen upon this artifice; and among those many paradoxicall and unheard of imitations, should not attempt to make one speak. The Serpent that spake unto Eve, the Dogs and Cats, that usually speak unto Witches, might afford some encouragement. And since broad and thick chops are required in birds that speak, since lips and teeth are also organs of speech; from these there is also an advantage in quadrupedes; and a proximity of reason in Elephants and Apes above them all. Since also an Echo will speak without any mouth at all, articulately returning the voice of man, by only ordering the vocall spirit in concave and hollow places; whether the musculous and motive parts about the hollow mouthes of beasts, may not dispose the passing spirit into some articulate notes, seems a querie of no great doubt.

Of the Badger

That a Brock or Badger hath the legs of one side shorter then of the other, though an opinion perhaps not very ancient, is yet very generall; received not only by theorists and unexperienced beleevers, but assented unto by most who have the opportunity to behold and hunt them daily. Which notwithstanding upon enquiry I finde repugnant unto the three determinators of truth, Authority, Sense and Reason. For first, Albertus *magnus* speaks dubiously, confessing he could not confirm the verity hereof; but Aldrovand affirmeth plainly, there can be no such inequality observed. And for my own part, upon indifferent enquiry, I cannot discover this difference; although the regardible side be defined, and the brevity by most imputed unto the left.

Again, It seems no easie affront unto reason, and generally repugnant unto the course of nature; for if we survey the totall set of animals, we may in their legs, or organs of progression, observe an equality of length, and parity of numeration; that is, not any to have an odde leg, or the supporters and movers of one side not exactly answered by the other. Although the hinder may be unequall unto the fore and middle legs, as in Frogs, Locusts and Grashoppers; or both unto the middle, as in some beetles, and spiders, as is determined by Aristotle *de incessu animalium.* Perfect and viviparous quadrupeds, so standing in their position of pronenesse, that the opposite joints of neighbour legs consist in the same plane; and a line descending from their navell interesects at right angles the axis of the earth. It happeneth often I confesse that a Lobster hath the chely or great claw of one side longer then the other; but this is not properly their legs, but a part of apprehension, and whereby they hold or seize upon their prey; for the legs and proper parts of progression are inverted backward, and stand in a position opposite unto these.

Lastly, The monstrosity is ill contrived, and with some disadvantage; the shortnesse being affixed unto the legs of one side, which might have been more tolerably placed upon the thwart or Diagoniall movers; for the progression of quadrupeds being performed *per Diametrum*, that is the crosse legs moving or resting together, so that two are alwaies in motion, and two in station at the same time; the brevity had been more tolerable in the crosse legs. For then the motion and station had been performed by equall legs; whereas herein they are both performed by unequall organs, and the imperfection becomes discoverable at every hand.

Of the Unicorns horn

Great account and much profit is made of Unicorns horn, at least of that which beareth the name thereof; wherein notwithstanding, many I perceive suspect an Imposture, and some conceive there is no such animall extant. Herein therefore to draw up our determinations, beside the severall places of Scripture mentioning this animall (which some perhaps may contend to be only meant of the Rhinoceros) we are so far from denying there is any

Unicorn at all, that we affirm there are many kindes thereof. In the number of Quadrupedes, we will concede no lesse then five; that is, the Indian Oxe, the Indian Asse, the Rhinoceros, the Oryx, and that which is more eminently termed *Monoceros*, or *Unicornis*: Some in the list of fishes; as that described by Olaus, Albertus and others: and some unicorns we will allow even among insects; as those four kindes of nasicornous Beetles described by Mussetus.

Secondly, Although we concede there be many Unicornes, yet are we still to seek; for whereunto to affix this horn in question, or to determine from which thereof we receive this magnified medicine, we have no assurance, or any satisfactory decision. For although we single out one, and eminently thereto assigne the name of the Unicorn, yet can we not be secure what creature is meant thereby, what constant shape it holdeth, or in what number to be received. For as far as our endeavours discover, this animall is not uniformly described, but differently set forth by those that undertake it . . .

Thirdly, Although we were agreed what animall this was, or differed not in its description, yet would this also afford but little satisfaction; for the horne we commonly extoll, is not the same with that of the Ancients; for that in the description of Ælian and Pliny was black; this which is shewed amongst us is commonly white, none black; and of those five which Scaliger beheld, though one spadiceous, or of a light red, and two inclining to red, yet was there not any of this complexion among them.

Fourthly, What horns soever they be which passe

amongst us, they are not surely the horns of any one kinde of animall, but must proceed from severall sorts of Unicorns . . .

Fifthly, Although there be many Unicorns, and consequently many horns, yet many there are which bear that name, and currantly passe among us, which are no horns at all . . .

Sixtly, Although we were satisfied we had the Unicornes horn, yet were it no injury unto reason to question the efficacy thereof, or whether those vertues pretended doe properly belong unto it. For what we observe (and it escaped not the observation of Paulus Jovius many years past) none of the Ancients ascribed any medicinall or antidotall vertue unto the Unicorns horn; and that which Ælian extolleth, who was the first and only man of the Ancients who spake of the medicall vertue of any Unicorn, was the horn of the Indian Asse; whereof, saith he, the Princes of those parts make bowles and drink therein, as preservatives against poison, Convulsions and the Falling-sicknesse. Now the description of that horn is not agreeable unto that we commend; for that (saith he) is red above, white below, and black in the middle; which is very different from ours, or any to be seen amongst us. And thus, though the description of the Unicorn be very ancient, yet was there of old no vertue ascribed unto it; and although this amongst us receive the opinion of the same vertue, yet is it not the same horn whereunto the Ancients ascribed it . . . Since therefore there be many Unicornes; Since that whereto we appropriate a horn is so variously described, that it seemeth either never to have been seen by two persons, or not to have been one animall; Since though they agreed in the description of the animall, yet is not the horn we extoll the same with that of the Ancients; Since what hornes soever they be that passe among us, they are not the hornes of one, but severall animals: Since many in common use and high esteem are no hornes at all: Since if they were true hornes, yet might their vertues be questioned: Since though we allowed some vertues, yet were not others to be received; with what security a man may rely on this remedy, the mistresse of fools hath already instructed some, and to wisdome (which is never too wise to learn) it is not too late to consider.

Of Sperma-Ceti, and the Sperma-Ceti Whale

What Sperma-Ceti is, men might justly doubt, since the learned *Hofmannus* in his work of Thirty years, saith plainly, *Nescio quid sit*.* And therefore need not wonder at the variety of opinions; while some conceived it to be *flos maris*, and many, a bituminous substance floating upon the sea.

That it was not the spawn of the Whale, according to vulgar conceit, or nominal appellation, Phylosophers have always doubted; not easily conceiving the Seminal humour of Animals, should be inflammable; or of a floating nature.

That it proceedeth from the Whale, beside the relation of *Clusius* and other learned observers, was indubitably

* I do not know what it is.

determined, not many years since by a Sperma-Ceti
Whale, cast on our coast of *Norfolk*. Which, to lead on
further inquiry, we cannot omit to inform. It contained
no less then sixty foot in length, the head somewhat
peculiar, with a large prominency over the mouth; teeth
only in the lower Jaw, received into fleshly sockets in
the upper. The Weight of the largest about two pound:
No gristly substances in the mouth, commonly called
Whale-bones; Only two short finns seated forwardly
on the back; the eyes but small, the pizell large, and
prominent. A lesser Whale of this kind above twenty
years ago, was cast up on the same shore.

The description of this Whale seems omitted by
Gesner, Rondeletius, and the first Editions of *Aldrovandus;*
but described in the latin impression of *Pareus,* in the
Exoticks of *Clusius,* and the natural history of *Niremberg-
ius,* but more amply in the Icons and figures of *Johnstonus.*

Mariners (who are not the best Nomenclators) called
it a *Jubartas,* or rather *Gibbartus.* Of the same appellation
we meet with one in *Rondeletius,* called by the *French*
Gibbar, from its round and gibbous back. The name
Gibbarta we find also given unto one kind of *Greenland*
Whales: But this of ours seemed not to answer the Whale
of that denomination; but more agreeable unto the
Trumpa or Sperma-Ceti Whale: according to the account
of our *Greenland* describers in *Purchas.* And maketh the
third among the eight remarkable Whales of that Coast.

Out of the head of this Whale, having been dead
divers daies, and under putrifaction, flowed streams of
oyl and Sperma-Ceti; which was carefully taken up and
preserved by the Coasters. But upon breaking up, the

Magazin of Sperma-Ceti, was found in the head lying in foulds and courses, in the bigness of goose eggs, encompassed with large flakie substances, as large as a mans head, in form of hony-combs, very white and full of oyl.

Some resemblance or trace hereof there seems to be in the *Physiter* or *Capidolio* of *Rondeletius*; while he delivers, that a fatness more liquid then oyl, runs from the brain of that animal; which being out, the Reliques are like the skales of *Sardinos* pressed into a mass; which melting with heat, are again concreted by cold. And this many conceive to have been the fish which swallowed *Jonas*. Although for the largeness of the mouth, and frequency in those seas, may possibly be the *Lamia*.*

Some part of the Sperma-Ceti found on the shore was pure, and needed little depuration; a great part mixed with fetid oyl, needing good preparation, and frequent expression, to bring it to a flakie consistency. And not only the head, but other parts contained it. For the carnous parts being roasted, the oyl dropped out, an axungious and thicker part subsiding; the oyl it self contained also much in it, and still after many years some is obtained from it.

Greenland Enquirers seldom meet with a Whale of this kind: and therefore it is but a contingent Commodity, not reparable from any other. It flameth white and candent like Champhire, but dissolveth not in *aqua fortis*, like it. Some lumps containing about two ounces, kept ever since in water, afford a fresh, and flosculous smell.

---

* [A kind of shark.]

Well prepared and separated from the oyl, it is of a substance unlikely to decay, and may outlast the oyl required in the Composition of *Mathiolus*.

Of the large quantity of oyl, what first came forth by expression from the *Sperma-Ceti*, grew very white and clear, like that of Almonds or Ben. What came by decoction was red. It was found to spend much in the vessels which contained it: It freezeth or coagulateth quickly with cold, and the newer soonest. It seems different from the oyl of any other animal, and very much frustrated the expectation of our soap-boylers, as not incorporating or mingling with their lyes. But it mixeth well with painting Colours, though hardly drieth at all. Combers of wool made use hereof, and Country people for cuts, aches and hard tumors. It may prove of good Medical use; and serve for a ground in compounded oyls and Balsams. Distilled, it affords a strong oyl, with a quick and piercing water. Upon Evaporation it gives a balsame, which is better performed with Turpentine distilled with *Sperma-Ceti*.

Had the abominable scent permitted, enquirie had been made into that strange composure of the head, and hillock of flesh about it. Since the workmen affirmed, they met with *Sperma-Ceti* before they came to the bone, and the head yet preserved, seems to confirm the same. The sphincters inserving unto the Fistula or spout, might have been examined, since they are so notably contrived in other cetaceous Animals; as also the Larynx or Throtle, whether answerable unto that of Dolphins and Porposes in the strange composure and figure which it maketh. What figure the stomack maintained in this Animal of one jaw of teeth, since in Porposes which abound in both, the ventricle is trebly divided, and since in that formerly taken nothing was found but weeds and a Loligo.* The heart, lungs, and kidneys, had no escaped; wherein are remarkable differences from Animals of the land, likewise what humor the bladder contained, but especially the seminal parts, which might have determined the difference of that humor, from this which beareth its name.

In vain it was to rake for Ambergreece in the panch of this *Leviathan*, as *Greenland* discoverers, and attests of experience dictate, that they sometimes swallow great lumps thereof in the Sea; insufferable fetour denying that enquiry. And yet if, as *Paracelsus* encourageth, Ordure makes the best Musk, and from the most fetid substances may be drawn the most odoriferous Essences; all that had not *Vespasians* Note, might boldly swear, here was a subject fit for such extractions.

Of the Picture of Adam and Eve with Navels

Another mistake there may be in the Picture of our first Parents, who after the manner of their posterity are both delineated with a Navell. And this is observable not only in ordinary and stained peeces, but in the Authentick draughts of Urbin, Angelo and others. Which notwithstanding cannot be allowed, except we impute that unto the first cause, which we impose not on the second; or

---

* [Squid.]

what we deny unto nature, we impute unto Naturity it self; that is, that in the first and most accomplished peece, the Creator affected superfluities, or ordained parts without all use or office.

For the use of the Navell is to continue the infant unto the Mother, and by the vessels thereof to convey its aliment and sustentation. The vessels whereof it consisteth, are the umbilicall vein, which is a branch of the Porta, and implanted in the liver of the Infant; two Arteries likewise arising from the Iliacall branches, by which the Infant receiveth the purer portion of bloud and spirits from the mother; and lastly, the Urachos or ligamentall passage derived from the bottome of the bladder, whereby it dischargeth the waterish and urinary part of its aliment. Now upon the birth when the Infant forsaketh the wombe, although it dilacerate, and break the involving membranes, yet doe these vessels hold, and by the mediation thereof the Infant is connected unto the wombe, not only before, but a while also after the birth. These therefore the midwife cutteth off, contriving them into a knot close unto the body of the Infant; from whence ensueth that tortuosity or complicated nodosity we usually call the Navell; occasioned by the colligation of vessels before mentioned. Now the Navell being a part, not precedent, but subsequent unto generation, nativity or parturition, it cannot be well imagined at the creation or extraordinary formation of Adam, who immediately issued from the Artifice of God; nor also that of Eve; who was not solemnly begotten, but suddenly framed, and anomalously proceeded from Adam.

And if we be led into conclusions that Adam had also this part, because we behold the same in our selves, the inference is not reasonable; for if we conceive the way of his formation, or of the first animals, did carry in all points a strict conformity unto succeeding productions, we might fall into imaginations that Adam was made without Teeth; or that he ran through those notable alterations in the vessels of the heart, which the Infant suffereth after birth: we need not dispute whether the egge or Bird were first; and might conceive that Dogges were created blinde, because we observe they are litered so with us. Which to affirm, is to confound, at least to regulate creation unto generation, the first Acts of God, unto the second of Nature, which were determined in that generall indulgence, Encrease and multiply, produce or propagate each other; that is, not answerably in all points, but in a prolonged method according to seminall progression. For the formation of things at first was different from their generation after; and although it had nothing to precede it, was aptly contrived for that which should succeed it. And therefore though Adam were framed without this part, as having no other wombe then that of his proper principles, yet was not his posterity without the same: for the seminality of his fabrick contained the power thereof; and was endued with the science of those parts whose pre-destinations upon succession it did accomplish.

All the Navell therefore and conjunctive part we can suppose in Adam, was his dependency on his Maker, and the connexion he must needs have unto heaven, who was the Sonne of God. For holding no dependence on any preceding efficient but God; in the act of his production there may be conceived some connexion, and Adam to have been in a moment all Navell with his Maker. And although from his carnality and corporall existence, the conjunction seemeth no nearer then of causality and effect; yet in his immortall and diviner part he seemed to hold a nearer coherence, and an umbilicality even with God himself. And so indeed although the propriety of this part be found but in some animals, and many species there are which have no Navell at all; yet is there one link and common connexion, one generall ligament, and necessary obligation of all whatever unto God. Whereby although they act themselves at distance, and seem to be at loose; yet doe they hold a continuity with their Maker. Which catenation or conserving union when ever his pleasure shall divide, let goe, or separate; they shall fall from their existence, essence, and operations; in brief, they must retire unto their primitive nothing, and shrink into that Chaos again . . .

They who hold the egge was before the Bird, prevent this doubt in many other animals, which also extendeth unto them; for Birds are nourished by umbilicall vessels, and the Navell is manifest sometimes a day or two after exclusion; the same is probable in all oviparous exclusions, if the lesser part of egges must serve for the formation, the greater part for nutriment. The same is made out in the egges of Snakes; and is not improbable in the generation of Porwiggles or Tadpoles; and may be also true in some vermiparous exclusions; although (as we have observed the daily progresse thereof) the whole Maggot is little enough to make a Flye, without any part remaining.